Come and Worship

Ways to Worship
from the HEBREW Scriptures

Magnified and sanctified be His great name in the world which He has created according to His will. May He establish His kingdom during your life and during your days, and during the life of the whole house of Israel, even swiftly and soon, and say amen.

Let His great name be blessed forever and to all eternity.

Blessed, praised, and glorified, exalted, extolled and honored, magnified and lauded be the name of the Holy One, blessed is He, though He be high above all the blessings and songs, praises, and consolations which are uttered in the world, and say amen.

May He Who makes peace in His high places make peace upon us and upon all Israel, and say amen.*

Dedication

My heart's desire and hope of my life is that Adonai will bring all believers everywhere
into a deeper more intimate relationship with him through praise and worship.
If he chooses to use this book I will be honored.
Praise him!

The Kadeesh, from the Messianic Shabbat Siddur compiled by Jeremiah Greenberg, page 62, 2001.

Come and Worship

Ways to Worship
from the HEBREW Scriptures

Compiled by Barbara D. Malda

Lederer Books
a division of
Messianic Jewish Publishers
Clarksville, Maryland

16 15 14 13   4 3 2 1

ISBN-13: 978-1-936716-67-8
ISBN-10: 1-936716-67-4

Library of Congress Control Number: 2013940888
Printed in the United States of America

Lederer Books
A division of
Messianic Jewish Publishers
6120 Day Long Lane
Clarksville, MD 21029

Distributed by
Messianic Jewish Resources Int'l
Order line: (800) 410-7367
lederer@messianicjewish.net
www.messianicjewish.net

CONTENTS

This book is divided into nine parts, each one being a Hebrew word for praise. The scriptures have been compiled to support these headings. From silence to antiphonal choirs of hundreds, from functioning in his gifts to walking in his fruit, from heart attitude to outward show, all of our worship is hinged on faith, how we walk, see, hear, and think is all colored by our trust in him and how deep a trust that is.

Guide for Pronunciation of Hebrew Transliteration

An effort has been made to conform to modern Israeli pronunciation of Hebrew.
We have adhered to the pronunciation guide below,
except in cases where convention has rendered a standard spelling.

- "a" is pronounced "ah" as in "hurrah"
- "ai" is pronounced "uy" as in "buy"
- "e" is pronounced "eh" as in "get"
- "ey" is pronounced "ay" as in "day"
- "i" is pronounced "ee" as in "see"
- "u" is pronounced "oo" as in "soon"
- "kh" and "ch" have no actual English equivalent;
they are gutteral sounds, which are made in the back of the throat

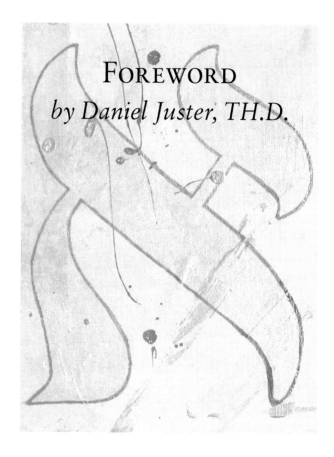

FOREWORD
by Daniel Juster, TH.D.

Eight years ago, when I wrote the foreword for *His Names are Wonderful*, the first book by Barbara Malda and Elizabeth Vander Meulen, little did I know the impact this book would have. People all over the world have learned the Hebrew names for God and have gotten to know the Lord of the Universe better. It's through God's various names that he is revealed.

In this follow-up work to *His Names are Wonderful*, Barbara Malda has once again enabled us to learn more because of her understanding of Hebrew, the original language of over 80% of the bible. This time, she chose to compile and arrange many verses of scripture that pertain to worship in *Come and Worship: Ways to Worship from the Hebrew Scriptures*.

Worship has transforming power. It brings the very presence of the *Ruach*, the Spirit. So if such passages are used as part of worship, it will result in growth. Generally, I do not know of such a work that simply and clearly compiles with good art, the Scriptural material on worship: its centrality, its variety, and its depth.

People often ask, "How do I worship God?" They try through a variety of means—worship services, reading devotionals, talking to him. These approaches are given in Scripture and have enabled billions of people to give praise to the Almighty. But, some ways of worship have been missed. In this little book, we are provided with an organized compilation of verses that show us ways to worship taken solely from the Hebrew Scriptures.

This is another really wonderful devotional book that will lead us to deeper worship. I hope many enjoy it. I will certainly be recommending this book to all who inquire about biblical worship.

God Bless,
Rabbi Dr. Daniel Juster, President
Tikkun International
May, 2013

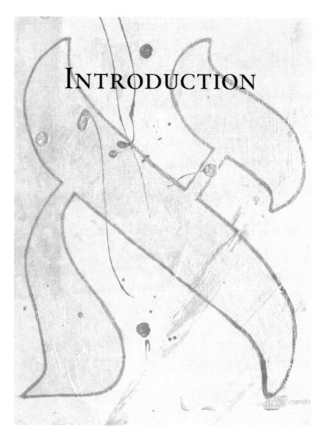

INTRODUCTION

"Sh'ma, Yisra'el! Adonai Eloheinu, Adonai echad [Hear, Isra'el! Adonai our God, Adonai is one]; and you are to love Adonai your God with all your heart, all your being and all your resources. These words, which I am ordering you today, are to be on your heart" (D'varim [Deut] 6:4–6).

When Moshe came down from Mount Sinai with the two tablets of the testimony in his hand, he didn't realize that the skin of his face was sending out rays of light as a result of his talking with [Adonai] (Exod 34:29).

We are called to be light, and when we are filled with holy anointing oil (the Ruach HaKodesh), we will give light to the space in front of us like the menorah. When we allow the things of the world to make our oil dirty, our light grows dim. As we worship Adonai, we must have pure oil, and shine brightly for him. Worship not only blesses our wonderful God, it blesses those around us, and ourselves.

We need to keep well oiled and shine brightly because worship is central to our being. We were created to worship and God has graciously given us many ways to express our praise to him. Each way fits a different situation or moment in life. Ecclessiates explains that there is a time for everything just as each form of worship has its place. Some expressions may be quiet or meditative, and others may be loud and expressive, but all are intended to bring honor and glory to him. When we believe that he is who he says he is [see previous book *His Names Are Wonderful*] and that his Word is true, worship flows naturally from our hearts to his.

The cause for our worship is summed up in the Siddur.*

"There is none like You among the gods, O Lord, and there is nothing like Your works. Your kingdom is an everlasting kingdom, and Your dominion is throughout all generations. The Lord reigns, the Lord has reigned, the Lord will reign for ever and ever. The Lord will give strength unto His people, the Lord will bless His people with peace."

Barbara Malda

Ayn Kamocha, from the Messianic Shabbat Siddur compiled by Jeremiah Greenberg, page 64, 2001.

1

BARAK

to bless, kneel down, show adoration, or salute

בָּרַךְ

Bowing Down

Genesis 24:26

The man bowed his head and prostrated himself before Adonai.

Exodus 4:31

The people believed; when they heard that Adonai had remembered the people of Isra'el and seen how they were oppressed, they bowed their heads and worshipped.

Exodus 34:8

At once Moshe bowed his head to the ground, prostrated himself and said, "If I have now found favor in your view, Adonai, then please let Adonai go with us, even though they are a stiffnecked people; and pardon our offenses and our sin; and take us as your possession."

1 Kings 18:42

Ach'av went up to eat and drink, while Eliyahu went up to the top of the Karmel. He bowed down to the ground and put his face between his knees.

Psalm 99:9

Exalt Adonai our God,
bow down toward his holy mountain,
for Adonai our God is holy!

Luke 24:50

He led them out toward Beit-Anyah; then, raising his hands, he said a b'rakhah over them; and as he was blessing them, he withdrew from them and was carried up into heaven. They bowed in worship to him, then returned to Yerushalayim, overflowing with joy.

(to bend the knee and position one's self in humility before a Holy God, thus raising him up and coming under his authority)

Judges 7:15

When Gid'on heard the dream and its interpretation, he fell on his knees in worship.

2 Chronicles 6:13–14

For Shlomo had made a bronze platform . . . and had set it up in the middle of the courtyard. He stood on it, then got down on his knees before the whole community, spread out his hands toward heaven, and said, "Adonai, God of Isra'el, there is no God like you in heaven or on earth."

Ezra 9:5–6

At the evening offering, with my cloak and tunic torn, I got up from afflicting myself, fell on my knees, spread out my hands to Adonai my God, and said, "My God, I am ashamed. I blush to lift my face to you, my God! For our sins tower over our heads; our guilt reaches up to heaven."

Psalm 95:6

Come, let's bow down and worship; let's kneel before Adonai who made us.

Ephesians 3:14–15

For this reason, I fall on my knees before the Father, from whom every family in heaven and on earth receives its character.

Prostrate/Face Down

(lying with the face down in demonstration of great humility or abject submission before the I AM That I AM and being completely overcome by who he is)

Genesis 24:52
When Avraham's servant heard what they said, he prostrated himself on the ground to Adonai.

Exodus 33:10
When all the people saw the column of cloud stationed at the entrance to the tent, they would get up and prostrate themselves, each man at his tent door.

Deuteronomy 9:25
"So I fell down before Adonai for those forty days and nights; and I lay there; because Adonai had said he would destroy you."

Deuteronomy 26:10–11
Therefore, as you see, I have now brought the firstfruits of the land which you, Adonai, have given me. You are then to put the basket down before Adonai your God, prostrate yourself before Adonai your God, and take joy in all the good that Adonai your God has given you, your household, the Levi and the foreigner living with you.

Joshua 7:6
Y'hoshua tore his clothes and fell to his face on the ground before the ark of Adonai until evening, he and the leaders of Isra'el, and they put dust on their heads.

Psalm 99:5
Prostrate yourselves at his footstool (he is holy).

Matthew 28:9
Suddenly Yeshua met them and said, "*Shalom*!" They came up and took hold of his feet as they fell down in front of him.

*(fully unpretentious, having an unassuming character or absence
of pride concerning the High, Exalted One's ways)*

2 Samuel 7:18

Then David went in, sat before Adonai and said, "Who am I, Adonai Elohim; and what is my family, that has caused you to bring me this far?"

2 Chronicles 7:14

. . . then, if my people, who bear my name, will humble themselves, pray, seek my face and turn from their evil ways, I will hear from heaven, forgive their sin and heal their land.

Isaiah 29:19

The humble will again rejoice in Adonai and the poor exult in the Holy One of Isra'el.

Isaiah 66:2

"Didn't I myself make all these things? This is how they all came to be," says Adonai. "The kind of person on whom I look with favor is one with a poor and humble spirit, who trembles at my word."

Daniel 10:12

Then he said to me, "Don't be afraid, Dani'el; because since the first day that you determined to understand and to humble yourself before your God, your words have been heard; and I have come because of what you said."

Matthew 18:4

So the greatest in the Kingdom is whoever makes himself as humble as this child.

1 Peter 5:6

Therefore, humble yourselves under the mighty hand of God, so that at the right time he may lift you up.

Trembling in His Presence

*(an actual physical shaking when our sinful flesh is overwhelmed
by the holy presence of Adonai our Refiner)*

Exodus 19:16
On the morning of the third day, there was thunder, lightning, and a thick cloud on the mountain. Then a shofar blast sounded so loudly that all the people in the camp trembled.

1 Chronicles 16:30
Tremble before him, all the earth!

Psalm 2:11
Serve Adonai with fear; rejoice, but with trembling.

Psalm 96:9
Worship Adonai in holy splendor; tremble before him, all the earth!

Psalm 99:1
Adonai is king; let the peoples tremble. He sits enthroned on the k'ruvim; let the earth shake!

Jeremiah 5:22
Don't you fear me?—says Adonai. Won't you tremble at my presence?

Joel 2:1
Blow the shofar in Tziyon! Sound an alarm on my holy mountain! Let all living in the land tremble, for the Day of Adonai is coming! It's upon us!

Ephesians 6:5
Slaves, obey your human masters with the same fear, trembling and single-heartedness with which you obey the Messiah.

Acts 7:32
"I am the God of your fathers, the God of Avraham, Yitz'chak and Ya'akov." But Moshe trembled with fear and didn't dare to look.

Taking Refuge or Hiding in Him

(utter abandon of self to his covering and shelter and being safely concealed in our Stronghold's retreat by relying on his divine protection)

2 Samuel 22:31

"As for God, his way is perfect, the word of Adonai has been tested by fire; he shields all who take refuge in him."

Psalm 27:5

For he will conceal me in his shelter on the day of trouble, he will hide me in the folds of his tent, he will set me high on a rock.

Psalm 57:2

Show me favor, God, show me favor; for in you I have taken refuge. Yes, I will find refuge in the shadow of your wings until the storms have passed.

Psalm 91:1–2, 4, 9

You who live in the shelter of Elyon, who spend your nights in the shadow of Shaddai, who say to Adonai, "My refuge! My fortress! My God, in whom I trust!" . . . he will cover you with his pinions, and under his wings you will find refuge. . . . For you have made Adonai, the Most High, who is my refuge, your dwelling-place.

Isaiah 49:2

He has made my mouth like a sharp sword while hiding me in the shadow of his hand; he has made me like a sharpened arrow while concealing me in his quiver.

Nahum 1:7

Adonai is good, a stronghold in time of trouble; he takes care of those who take refuge in him.

Colossians 3:3

For you have died, and your life is hidden with the Messiah in God.

BEING IN AWE OF HIM

(a mixed feeling of reverence, fear, and wonder caused by the greatness, superiority, and grandeur of the Greatness on High that takes our breath away)

Deuteronomy 4:10–11

The day you stood before Adonai your God at Horev, when Adonai said to me, "Gather the people to me, and I will make them hear my very words, so that they will learn to hold me in awe as long as they live on earth, and so that they will teach their children."

Psalm 33:8

Let all the earth fear Adonai! Let all living in the world stand in awe of him.

Psalm 65:9

This is why those living at the ends of the earth stand in awe of your signs. The places where the sun rises and sets you cause to sing for joy.

Isaiah 8:13

But Adonai-Tzva'ot—consecrate him! Let him be the object of your fear and awe!

Isaiah 29:23

When his descendants see the work of my hands among them, they will consecrate my name. Yes, they will consecrate the holy one of Ya'akov and stand in awe of the God of Isra'el.

Daniel 6:27

"I herewith issue a decree that everywhere in my kingdom, people are to tremble and be in awe of the God of Dani'el. For he is the living God; he endures forever. His kingdom will never be destroyed; his rulership will last till the end."

Matthew 15:30–31

And great crowds came to him. . . and he healed them so that the crowd wondered, when they saw the mute speaking the crippled healthy, the lame walking, and the blind seeing. And they glorified the God of Israel.

Revering Him

(a feeling or attitude of deep respect, love, and awe laced with loyalty to the Anointed One whom we hold dear)

1 Kings 18:3, 12

Ach'av called 'Ovadyah, who was in charge of the palace. Now 'Ovadyah greatly revered Adonai. . . . But as soon as I leave you, the Spirit of Adonai will carry you off to I don't know where; so that when I come and tell Ach'av, and he can't find you, he will kill me. But I your servant have revered Adonai from my youth.

Psalm 5:8

But I can enter your house because of your great grace and love; I will bow down toward your holy temple in reverence for you.

2 Corinthians 7:1

Therefore, my dear friends, since we have these promises, let us purify ourselves from everything that can defile either body or spirit, and strive to be completely holy, out of reverence for God.

Hebrews 12:28

Therefore, since we have received an unshakeable Kingdom, let us have grace, through which we may offer service that will please God, with reverence and fear.

Being Still, Quiet, or Silent

*(without sound, hushed, perfectly at rest, tranquil, calm,
respectfully waiting on the hand of the Master)*

Psalm 37:7

Be still before Adonai; wait patiently till he comes.

Psalm 62:6

My soul, wait in silence for God alone, because my hope comes from him.

Psalm 65:2

To you, God, in Tziyon, silence is praise; and vows to you are to be fulfilled.

Psalm 131:2

No, I keep myself calm and quiet, like a little child on its mother's lap—I keep myself like a little child.

Isaiah 26:16

Adonai, when they were troubled, they sought you. When you chastened them, they poured out a silent prayer.

Habakkuk 2:20

But Adonai is in his holy temple; let all the earth be silent before him.

Zephaniah 1:7

Keep silent before Adonai Elohim, for the Day of Adonai is near. Adonai has prepared a sacrifice; he has set apart those he invited.

Zechariah 2:17

Be silent, all humanity, before Adonai; for he has been roused from his holy dwelling.

Revelation 8:1

When the Lamb broke the seventh seal, there was silence in heaven for what seemed like half an hour.

FEARING HIM

***(respectful dread of his justice with a deep desire to please
the Ancient of Days out of reverence for him)***

1 Samuel 12:24

Only fear Adonai, and serve him faithfully with
all your heart; for think what great things he
has done for you!

Psalm 22:24

You who fear Adonai, praise him!

Psalm 34:10

Fear Adonai, you holy ones of his, for those
who fear him lack nothing.

Psalm 115:11

You who fear Adonai, trust in Adonai! He is
their help and shield.

Proverbs 3:7–8

Don't be conceited about your own wisdom; but
fear Adonai, and turn from evil. This will bring
health to your body and give strength to your
bones.

Ecclesiastes 12:13

Here is the final conclusion, now that you have
heard everything: fear God, and keep his *mitzvot*; this is what being human is all about.

Luke 12:5

I will show you whom to fear: fear him who
after killing you has authority to throw you
into Gei-Hinnom! Yes, I tell you, this is the one
to fear!

Revelation 14:7

In a loud voice he said, "Fear God, give him
glory, for the hour has come when he will pass
judgment! Worship the One who made heaven
and earth, the sea and the springs of water!"

Revelation 15:4

Adonai, who will not fear and glorify your
name? because you alone are holy.

2

YADAH

to revere or worship,
to throw out the hand,
give thanks,
praise, or lift the hands

יָדָה

STANDING

(showing agreement and immovable determination to perform God's will, acknowledge his greatness and to stand under him, our Banner)

Genesis 19:27

Avraham got up early in the morning, went to the place where he had stood before Adonai.

1 Samuel 6:20

The people of Beit-Shemesh asked, "Who can stand before Adonai, this holy God?"

Psalm 22:24

All descendants of Isra'el, stand in awe of him! Let all living in the world stand in awe of him.

Psalm 60:6–7

To those who fear you because of the truth you gave a banner to rally around, so that those you love could be rescued.

Psalm 84:11

Better a day in your courtyards than a thousand [days elsewhere]. Better just standing at the door of my God's house than living in the tents of the wicked.

Psalm 106:21–23

They forgot God . . . Therefore he said that he would destroy them, [and he would have] had not Moshe his chosen one stood before him in the breach to turn back his destroying fury.

Luke 21:19

By standing firm you will save your lives.

Ephesians 6:13–14

So take up every piece of war equipment God provides; so that when the evil day comes, you will be able to resist; and when the battle is won, you will still be standing. Therefore, stand!

LIFTING HANDS

(raising hands to any level to lift up his name, show surrender, or receive from our Sovereign God, petitioning, thanking, or praising him with our strength)

1 Kings 8:22

Then Shlomo stood before the altar of Adonai in the presence of the whole community of Isra'el, spread out his hands toward heaven, and said, "Adonai, God of Isra'el, there is no God like you in heaven above or on earth below."

Nehemiah 8:6

Ezra blessed Adonai, the great God; and all the people answered, "Amen! Amen!" as they lifted up their hands, bowed their heads and fell prostrate before Adonai with their faces to the ground.

Psalm 28:2

Hear the sound of my prayers when I cry to you, when I lift my hands toward your holy sanctuary.

Psalm 63:5

Yes, I will bless you as long as I live; in your name I will lift up my hands.

Psalm 77:3

On the day of my distress I am seeking Adonai; my hands are lifted up; my tears flow all night without ceasing; my heart refuses comfort.

Psalm 134:2

Lift your hands toward the sanctuary, and bless Adonai.

Lamentations 3:41

Let us lift up our hearts and our hands to God in heaven . . .

1 Timothy 2:8

Therefore, it is my wish that when the men pray, no matter where, they should lift up hands that are holy—they should not become angry or get into arguments.

Lifting Up Your face

(connecting with the presence of God, with our hearts fully focused on him and fixing our gaze on him causing our whole being to be attentive to the Only Wise God)

Ezra 9:6

"My God, I am ashamed. I blush to lift my face to you, my God! For our sins tower over our heads; our guilt reaches up to heaven."

Job 11:15

Then when you lift up your face, there will be no defect; you will be firm and free from fear.

Job 22:26

Then Shaddai will be your delight, you will lift up your face to God.

Psalm 17:15

But my prayer, in righteousness, is to see your face; on waking, may I be satisfied with a vision of you.

Psalm 27:8

My heart said of you, "See my face." Your face, Adonai, I will seek.

Matthew 14:19

After instructing the crowds to sit down on the grass, he took the five loaves and the two fish and, looking up toward heaven, made a b'rakhah.

Mark 7:34–35

. . . then, looking up to heaven, he gave a deep groan and said to him, "Hippatach!" (that is, "Be opened!") His ears were opened, his tongue was freed, and he began speaking clearly.

Acts 7:55

But he [Stephen], full of the Ruach HaKodesh, looked up to heaven and saw God's Sh'khinah, with Yeshua standing at the right hand of God.

Colossians 3:2

Focus your minds on the things above, not on things here on earth.

(to touch or caress gently and lightly with the lips as in kissing the Torah, a mezuzah, or our hand as we lift it up toward heaven to our Faithful One)

Psalm 2:12
Kiss the son, lest he be angry, and you perish along the way, when suddenly his anger blazes. How blessed are all who take refuge in him.

Song of Solomon 1:2
Let him smother me with kisses from his mouth, for your love is better than wine.

Song of Solomon 4:11
Your lips, my bride, drip honey; honey and milk are under your tongue; and the scent of your garments is like the scent of the L'vanon.

Song of Solomon 5:13
His cheeks are like beds of spices, like banks of frangrant herbs. His lips are like lilies dripping with sweet myrrh.

Luke 7:38
A woman who lived in that town, a sinner, who was aware that he was eating in the home of the *Parush* [Pharisee], brought an alabaster box of very expensive perfume, stood behind Yeshua at his feet and wept until her tears began to wet his feet. Then she wiped his feet with her own hair, kissed his feet and poured the perfume on them.

Luke 7:45
You didn't give me a kiss; but from the time I arrived, this woman has not stopped kissing my feet!

Being Intimate with Him

(a totally honest knowing of his inmost character and sharing uninterrupted focused time gazing at our Beloved with a heart intensely yearning to grow closer to him)

Psalm 139:1–4

Adonai, you have probed me, and you know me. You know when I sit and when I stand up, you discern my inclinations from afar, you scrutinize my daily activities. You are so familiar with all my ways that before I speak even a word, Adonai, you know all about it already.

Proverbs 8:17

I love those who love me; and those who seek me will find me.

Song of Solomon 2:4

He brings me to the banquet hall; his banner over me is love. Sustain me with raisins, refresh me with apples, for I am sick with love.

John 10:14

I am the good shepherd; I know my own, and my own know me—just as the father knows me, and I know the father.

Ephesians 2:4

But God is so rich in mercy and loves us with such intense love that, even when we were dead because of our acts of disobedience, he brought us to life along with the Messiah—it is by grace that you have been delivered.

Ephesians 5:26–27

. . . in order to set it apart for God, making it clean through immersion in the *mikveh* [ritual bath with running water], so to speak, in order to present the Messianic Community to himself as a bride to be proud of, without a spot, wrinkle or any such thing, but holy and without defect.

(to hold fast by embracing, or stubbornly grasping as if our lives depend on it, and refusing to let go of God With Us)

Deuteronomy 10:20

You are to fear Adonai your God, serve him, cling to him and swear by his name.

Deuteronomy 13:5

You are to follow Adonai your God, fear him, obey his *mitzvot* [commands], listen to what he says, serve him and cling to him.

Deuteronomy 30:20

. . . loving Adonai your God, paying attention to what he says and clinging to him—for that is the purpose of your life!

Joshua 22:5

"Only take great care to obey the *mitzvah* and the Torah which Moshe the servant of Adonai gave you—to love Adonai your God, follow all his ways, observe his *mitzvot*, cling to him, and serve him with all your heart and being."

2 Kings 18:6–7

For he clung to Adonai and did not leave off following him, but obeyed his *mitzvot*, which Adonai had given Moshe. So Adonai was with him.

Psalm 63:7–8

For you have been my help; in the shadow of your wings I rejoice; my heart clings to you; your right hand supports me.

Psalm 119:31

I cling to your instruction; Adonai, don't let me be put to shame!

Luke 8:15

As for that in the good soil, they are those who, hearing the word, hold it fast in an honest and good heart, and bear fruit with patience.

THANKING HIM

(to show or express appreciation or gratitude to our lavishly generous provider and protector and to acknowledge the gracious hand of the Giver)

Ezra 3:11

And they sang responsively, praising and giving thanks to the Lord,

> "For he is good,
> for his steadfast love endures forever
> toward Israel."

Psalm 75:2

We give thanks to you, God, we give thanks; your name is near, people tell of your wonders.

Psalm 86:11

Adonai, teach me your way, so that I can live by your truth; make me single-hearted, so that I can fear your name. I will thank you, Adonai my God, with my whole heart; and I will glorify your name forever.

Psalm 100:4

Enter his gates with thanksgiving, enter his courtyards with praise; give thanks to him, and bless his name.

Psalm 109:30

I will eagerly thank Adonai with my mouth, I will praise him right there in the crowd.

Psalm 119:7

I thank you with a sincere heart as I learn your righteous rulings.

Ephesians 5:20

Giving thanks always and for everything to God the Father in the name of our Lord Yeshua the Messiah.

(to adore, or revere the Enthroned One with extreme devotion, intense love, obedience and admiration becoming evident in every aspect of our lives)

1 Chronicles 16:29

Give Adonai the glory due to his name; bring an offering, and come into his presence. Worship Adonai in splendid, holy attire.

Psalm 22:28

All the ends of the earth will remember and turn to Adonai; all the clans of the nations will worship in your presence.

Psalm 29:2

. . . give Adonai the glory due his name; worship Adonai in holy splendor.

Psalm 63:4

For your grace is better than life. My lips will worship you.

Psalm 96:9

Worship Adonai in holy splendor; tremble before him, all the earth!

Matthew 2:1–2

Magi from the east came to Yerushalayim and asked, "Where is the newborn King of the Jews? For we saw his star in the east and have come to worship him."

John 4:23–24

But the time is coming—indeed, it's here now—when the true worshippers will worship the Father spiritually and truly, for these are the kind of people the Father wants worshipping him. God is spirit; and worshippers must worship him spiritually and truly.

Delighting in Him

(to take great joy or pleasure in or to be highly pleased with our God of Kindness, smiling inwardly with a glad heart when we think of all he's done)

Deuteronomy 26:11

. . . take joy in all the good that Adonai your God has given you, your household, the Levi and the foreigner living with you.

Psalm 1:2

Their delight is in Adonai's Torah; on his Torah they meditate day and night.

Psalm 16:11

You make me know the path of life; in your presence is unbounded joy, in your right hand eternal delight.

Psalm 35:27

But may those who delight in my righteousness shout for joy and be glad! Let them say always, "How great is Adonai, who delights in the peace of his servant!"

Psalm 37:4

Then you will delight yourself in Adonai, and he will give you your heart's desire.

Psalm 119:16

I will find my delight in your regulations. I will not forget your word.

Romans 7:22

For I delight in the law of God, in my inner being.

(to make evident and bring into focus the many faceted character of Adonai, looking closely into the Living Word and bringing to light the minutest detail of who he is)

2 Samuel 7:26

May your name be magnified forever, so that it will be said, "Adonai-Tzva'ot is God over Isra'el, and the dynasty of your servant David will be set up in your presence."

1 Chronicles 17:24

May your name be confirmed and magnified forever.

Job 36:24

Remember, rather, to magnify his work, of which many have sung.

Luke 1:46–48

Then Miryam said, "My soul magnifies Adonai; and my spirit rejoices in God, my Savior, who has taken notice of his servant-girl in her humble position."

James 1:25

But if a person looks closely into the perfect *Torah*, which gives freedom, and continues, becoming not a forgetful hearer but a doer of the work it requires, then he will be blessed in what
he does.

SEEKING HIM

(with our hearts and eyes wide open trying to find the Way, the Truth, and the Life; we aim at, pursue, or search for our God who loves to make himself known to us)

Deuteronomy 4:29

However, from there you will seek Adonai your God; and you will find him if you search after him with all your heart and being.

2 Chronicles 15:15

All Y'hudah was full of joy at his oath; for they had sworn with all their heart and had sought him with all their will; and they found him, and Adonai gave them rest all around.

Psalm 63:2

O God, you are my God; I will seek you eagerly. My heart thirsts for you, my body longs for you in a land parched and exhausted, where no water can be found.

Psalm 105:4

Seek Adonai and his strength; always seek his presence.

Isaiah 55:6

Seek Adonai while he is available, call on him while he is still nearby.

Jeremiah 29:13

"When you seek me, you will find me, provided you seek for me wholeheartedly; and I will let you find me," says Adonai.

Hebrews 11:6

And without trusting, it is impossible to be well pleasing to God, because whoever approaches him must trust that he does exist and that he becomes a Rewarder to those who seek him out.

(to be sure of or well informed as to who God is, and having a clear perception or understanding of him as he reveals himself through his creation and his Word)

Exodus 6:7

I will take you as my people, and I will be your God. Then you will know that I am Adonai your God, who freed you from the forced labor of the Egyptians.

Exodus 31:13

Tell the people of Isra'el, "You are to observe my Shabbats; for this is a sign between me and you through all your generations; so that you will know that I am Adonai, who sets you apart for me."

Ezekiel 37:28

The nations will know that I am Adonai, who sets Isra'el apart as holy, when my sanctuary is with them forever.

Ezekiel 38:23

I will show my greatness and holiness, making myself known in the sight of many nations; then they will know that I am Adonai.

Hosea 6:6

For what I desire is mercy, not sacrifices, knowledge of God more than burnt offerings.

Habbakuk 2:14

For the earth will be as full of the knowledge of Adonai's glory as water covering the sea.

John 17:3

And eternal life is this: to know you, the one true God, and him whom you sent, Yeshua the Messiah.

3

TEHILLAH

a song or hymn of praise,
a spontaneous expression
of a spiritual song,
or to laud, praise, honor,
or glorify the many facets
of Adonai

תְּחִלָּה

Praising Him

(to express approval or admiration, to laud the glory of the King of Kings as in song, to glorify, or extol using words of high praise)

Psalm 22:4

Nevertheless, you are holy, enthroned on the praises of Isra'el.

Psalm 40:4

He put a new song in my mouth, a song of praise to our God.

Psalm 66:2

Sing the glory of his name, make his praise glorious.

Psalm 102:19

May this be put on record for a future generation; may a people yet to be created to praise Adonai.

Psalm 145:3

Great is Adonai and greatly to be praised; his greatness is beyond all searching out. Each generation will praise your works to the next and proclaim your mighty acts.

Psalm 146:1–2

Halleluyah! Praise Adonai, my soul! I will praise Adonai as long as I live. I will sing praise to my God all my life.

Psalm 148:1

Halleluyah! Praise Adonai from the heavens! Praise him in the heights!

Psalm 150:6

Let everything that has breath praise Adonai! Halleluyah!

Revelation 19:5

And from the throne came a voice saying, "Praise our God, all you his servants, you who fear him, great and small."

(heartfelt praise given to glorify, or acknowledge his Holy Name and to exalt this name by proclaiming who he is with our words and our actions)

Genesis 24:48

Then I bowed my head and worshiped the Lord and blessed the Lord.

1 Chronicles 29:10

He blessed Adonai before the entire community: "Blessed be you, Adonai, the God of Isra'el our father, forever and ever."

2 Chronicles 20:26

On the fourth day, they assembled in the Valley of B'rakhah [blessing], where they blessed Adonai; hence that place is called the Valley of B'rakhah
to this day.

Nehemiah 9:5

"Blessed be your glorious name, exalted above all blessing and praise!"

Psalm 92:2

Sing to Adonai, bless his name! Proclaim his victory day after day!

Psalm 103:1

Bless Adonai, my soul! Everything in me, bless his holy name!

Psalm 145:2

Every day I will bless you; I will praise your name forever and ever.

Psalm 145:10

All your creatures will thank you, Adonai, and your faithful servants will bless you.

Ephesians 1:3

Blessed be the God and Father of our Lord Yeshua the Messiah, who has blessed us in Messiah with every spiritual blessing in the heavenly places.

Honoring Him

(having high regard or great respect to the Worthy One and showing this by giving him obedience, thanksgiving, offerings, glory, fame, renown, and dignity)

Exodus 5:1

After that, Moshe and Aharon came and said to Pharoah, "Here is what Adonai, the God of Isra'el says: 'Let my people go, so that they can celebrate a festival in the desert to honor me.'"

Exodus 35:2

On six days work is to be done, but the seventh day is to be a holy day for you, a Shabbat of complete rest in honor of Adonai.

Psalm 50:14–15, 23

"Offer thanksgiving as your sacrifice to God, pay your vows to the Most High, and call on me when you are in trouble; I will deliver you, and you will honor me." . . . "Whoever offers thanksgiving as his sacrifice honors me; and to him who goes the right way I will show the salvation of God."

Proverbs 3:9

Honor Adonai with your wealth and with the first fruits of all your income.

Proverbs 14:31

The oppressor of the poor insults his maker, but he who is kind to the needy honors him.

John 5:23

. . . so that all may honor the Son as they honor the Father. Whoever fails to honor the Son is not honoring the Father who sent him.

Philippians 1:20

It all accords with my earnest expectation and hope that I will have nothing to be ashamed of; but rather, now, as always, the Messiah will be honored by my body, whether it is alive or dead.

EXALTING HIM

(to raise on high, elevate or intensify our praise, to glorify or extol or lift up the Everlasting God and to be filled with sublime emotion or inspiring awe of him)

Exodus 15:21

. . . as Miryam sang to them: "Sing to Adonai, for he is highly exalted! The horse and its rider he threw in the sea!"

2 Samuel 22:47

"Adonai is alive! Blessed is my Rock! Exalted be God, the Rock of my salvation."

Job 36:22

Look, God is exalted in his strength; who is a teacher like him?

Psalm 148:13

Let them praise the name of Adonai, for his name alone is exalted; his glory is above both earth and heaven.

Isaiah 12:4

On that day you will say, "Give thanks to Adonai! Call on his name! Make his deeds known among the peoples, declare how exalted is his name."

Isaiah 25:1

Adonai, you are my God. I exalt you, I praise your name. For you have accomplished marvels, [fulfilled] ancient plans faithfully and truly.

Isaiah 33:5

Adonai is exalted, for he dwells on high; he has filled Tziyon with justice and righteousness.

Acts 2:33

"Moreover, he has been exalted to the right hand of God; has received from the Father what he promised, namely, the Ruach Ha-Kodesh; and has poured out this gift, which you are both seeing and hearing."

EXTOLING HIM

(to raise up, or praise extravagantly our Defender as with an outward show of strong approval through song, loud applause, or cheering)

Job 36:24
Remember to extol his work, of which men have sung.

Psalm 69:31
I will praise God's name with a song and extol him with thanksgiving.

Psalm 107:32
Let them extol him in the assembly of the people and praise him in the leaders' council.

Psalm 145:1
I will extol you, my God and King.

Daniel 4:37
Now I, Nebuchadnezzar, praise and extol and honor the King of heaven, for all his works are right and his ways are just.

Romans 15:11
And again, praise the Lord, all you Gentiles, and let all the peoples extol him.

GLORIFYING HIM

(to exalt, honor, and praise the King of the Nations without restraint because of how splendid, majestic, victorious and wonderful he is)

Psalm 86:12

I will thank you, Adonai my God, with my whole heart; and I will glorify your name forever.

Psalm 96:7–8

Give Adonai his due, you families from the peoples; give Adonai his due of glory and strength; give Adonai the glory due to his name; bring an offering, and enter his courtyards.

Psalm 147:12

Glorify Adonai, Yerushalayim! Praise your God, Tziyon!

Romans 15:5–6

And may God, the source of encouragement and patience, give you the same attitude among yourselves as the Messiah Yeshua had, so that with one accord and with one voice you may glorify the God and Father of our Lord Yeshua the Messiah.

1 Corinthians 6:19–20

Or don't you know that your body is a temple for the Ruach HaKodesh who lives inside you, whom you received from God? The fact is, you don't belong to yourselves; for you were bought at a price. So use your bodies to glorify God.

2 Corinthians 9:13

In offering this service you prove to these people that you glorify God by actually doing what your acknowledgment of the Good News of the Messiah requires, namely, sharing generously with them and with everyone.

SINGING

(to describe, rejoice, or celebrate with song or verse who Yah is and what he's done, and expressing thankfulness with our voices from our hearts to him)

Exodus 15:1–2
Then Moshe and the people of Isra'el sang this song to Adonai: "I will sing to Adonai, for he is highly exalted: the horse and its rider he threw in the sea. Yah is my strength and my song, and he has become my salvation."

Psalm 13:6
I will sing to Adonai, because he gives me even more than I need.

Psalm 40:4
He put a new song in my mouth, a song of praise to our God.

Psalm 42:9
By day Adonai commands his grace, and at night his song is with me as a prayer to the God of my life.

Psalm 57:8
My heart is steadfast, God, steadfast. I will sing and make music.

Psalm 66:2
Sing the glory of his name, make his praise glorious.

Psalm 100:2
Serve Adonai with gladness. Enter his presence with joyful songs.

Colossians 3:16
And be thankful—let the Word of the Messiah, in all its richness, live in you, as you teach and counsel each other in all wisdom, and as you sing psalms, hymns and spiritual songs with gratitude to God in your hearts.

CHOIRS

*(trained, highly skilled, orgainized, harmonious groups of singers
bringing grandeur to the Lord who is My Song)*

1 Chronicles 23:4–5
Of these . . . 4,000 were gatekeepers, and 4,000 sang praise to Adonai "with the instruments I made for the purpose of singing praise."

2 Chronicles 35:25
Yirmeyahu composed a lament for Yoshiyahu; and all the men and women singers have sung of Yoshiyahu in their laments till this day. They made singing them a law in Isra'el, and they are recorded in the Laments.

Ezra 2:65
They also had 200 male and female singers.

Ezra 3:11
They sang antiphonally, praising and giving "thanks to Adonai, for he is good, for his grace continues forever" toward Isra'el.

Nehemiah 12:24
The chiefs of the *L'vi'im* . . . with their kinsmen in an antiphonal choir, to praise and give thanks, in accordance with the order of David the man of God, choir opposite choir.

Nehemiah 12:31
And after that I brought the leaders of Y'hudah up onto the wall and appointed two large choirs to give thanks and to walk in procession.

Nehemiah 12:40
Thus stood the two choirs of those giving thanks in the house of God, with myself and half of the leaders with me.

Revelation 14:3
And they were singing a new song before the throne and before the four living creatures and before the elders.

Clapping

*(a joyous expression of praise, appreciation, or approval
by a slapping of the hands together to Our Creator)*

Psalm 47:2

Clap your hands, all you peoples! Shout to God
with cries of joy!

Psalm 98:8

Let the floods clap their hands; let the mountains sing together for joy before Adonai.

Isaiah 55:12

Yes, you will go out with joy, you will be led
forth in peace. As you come, the mountains
and hills will burst out into song, and all the
trees in the countryside will clap their hands.

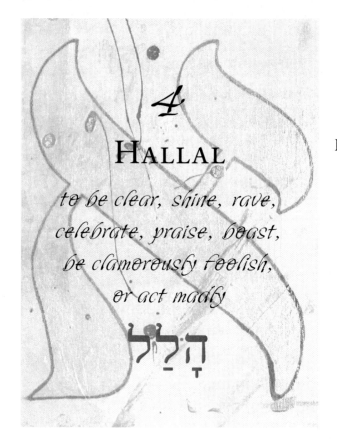

4

HALLAL

*to be clear, shine, rave,
celebrate, praise, boast,
be clamorously foolish,
or act madly*

הָלַל

LOVING ADONAI WITH ALL YOUR HEART

(a deep, all-consuming feeling of affection, attachment, or devotion fully focused on our gracious Redeemer who rescued us from darkness and sets us free from sin)

Deuteronomy 6:5
"And you are to love Adonai your God with all your heart, all your being and all your resources."

Deuteronomy 30:6
Then Adonai your God will circumcise your hearts and the hearts of your children, so that you will love Adonai your God with all your heart and all your being, and thus you will live.

Joshua 23:11
Therefore take great care to love Adonai your God.

1 Samuel 7:3
Sh'mu'el addressed all the people of Isra'el; he said: "If you are returning to Adonai with all your heart, then be done with the foreign gods and ashtarot that you have with you, and direct your hearts to Adonai."

Jeremiah 24:7
I will give them a heart to know me that I am Adonai. They will be my people, and I will be their God; for they will return to me with all their heart.

Matthew 22:37–39
He told him, "'You are to love Adonai your God with all your heart and with all your soul and with all your strength.' This is the greatest and most important *mitzvah*. And a second is similar to it, 'You are to love your neighbor as yourself.'"

1 Corinthians 8:3
However, if someone loves God, God knows him.

REJOICING IN HIM

*(to be glad, happy, or delighted, full of joy or a celebrative lightness
of spirit because we belong to the God of Our Praise)*

Psalm 33:1, 21

Rejoice in Adonai, you righteous! Praise is well-suited to the upright. . . . For in him our hearts rejoice, because we trust in his holy name.

Psalm 63:8

For you have been my help; in the shadow of your wings I rejoice.

Psalm 89:17–18

They rejoice in your name all day and are lifted up by your righteousness, for you yourself are the strength in which they glory.

Psalm 104:34

May my musings be pleasing to him; I will rejoice in Adonai.

Psalm 118:24

This is the day Adonai has made, a day for us to rejoice and be glad.

Psalm 149:2

Let Isra'el rejoice in their maker, let Tziyon's children take joy in their king.

Habakkuk 3:18

Still, I will rejoice in Adonai, I will take joy in the God of my salvation.

Zechariah 9:9

Rejoice with all your heart, daughter of Tziyon! Shout out loud, daughter of Yerushalayim! Look! Your king is coming to you. He is righteous, and he is victorious. Yet he is humble—he's riding on a donkey, yes, on a lowly donkey's colt.

Philippians 4:4

Rejoice in union with the Lord always! I will say it again: rejoice!

LAUGHING FOR JOY

(an outward release of happiness at our Prince of Peace and his victories,
and a deep inner gladness because of who he is and for his blessings and favor)

Genesis 21:6
Sarah said, "God has given me good reason to laugh; now everyone who hears about it will laugh with me."

Job 5:22
You'll be able to laugh at destruction and famine.

Job 8:21
He will yet fill your mouth with laughter and your lips with shouts of joy.

Job 22:19
The righteous saw this and rejoiced; the innocent laughed them to scorn.

Psalm 126:2
Our mouths were full of laughter, and our tongues shouted for joy.

Proverbs 31:25
Clothed with strength and dignity, she can laugh at the days to come.

Eccleciastes 3:4
. . . a time to weep and a time to laugh.

Luke 6:21
"How blessed are you who are hungry! for you will be filled. How blessed are you who are crying now! for you will laugh."

(the marking of God's feasts with ceremony or festivity in remembrance of what our Faithful Father has done for us, and obeying God's command to joyously celebrate them)

Exodus 12:14

"This will be a day for you to remember and celebrate as a festival to Adonai; from generation to generation you are to celebrate it by a perpetual regulation." [Pesach]

Exodus 20:8

Remember the day, *Shabbat*, to set it apart for God.

Leviticus 23:9–10

"You shall bring the sheaf of the firstfruits of your harvest to the priest, and he shall wave the sheaf before the Lord, so that you may be accepted." [Firstfruits]

Leviticus 23:23–24

"In the seventh month, on the first day of the month, you shall observe a day of solemn rest, a memorial proclaimed with blast of trumpets, a holy convocation." [Yom Teru'ah]

Leviticus 23:26

"Now on the tenth day of this seventh month is the Day of Atonement. It shall be for you a time of holy convocation." [Yom Kippur]

Leviticus 23:40, 42

On the first day you are to take choice fruit, palm fronds, thick branches and river-willows, and celebrate in the presence of Adonai your God for seven days. . . . You shall dwell in booths for seven days. [Sukkot]

1 Corinthians 5:8

So let us celebrate the Seder not with leftover hametz, the hametz of wickedness and evil, but with the matzah of purity and truth. [Pesach]

Being Glad in Him

(a joyful elation or a deep sense of gratification, contentment, mirth, or inner cheer because of our Shepherd's presence and being happily assured of who he is)

1 Chronicles 16:31
Let the heavens rejoice; let the earth be glad; let them say among the nations, "Adonai is king!"

Psalm 5:12
But let all who take refuge in you rejoice, let them forever shout for joy! Shelter them; and they will be glad, those who love your name.

Psalm 31:8
I will rejoice and be glad in your grace, for you see my affliction, you know how distressed I am.

Psalm 32:11
Be glad in Adonai; rejoice, you righteous! Shout for joy, all you upright in heart!

Psalm 34:3
When I boast, it will be about Adonai; the humble will hear of it and be glad.

Psalm 70:5
But may all those who seek you be glad and take joy in you. May those who love your salvation say always, "God is great and glorious!"

Psalm 118:24
This is the day Adonai has made, a day for us to rejoice and be glad.

Matthew 5:12
Rejoice, be glad, because your reward in heaven is great—they persecuted the prophets before you in the same way.

(to move the body to music to express love for or joy in our Hope that words cannot express, and to worship with all our might or to celebrate with abandon)

1 Samuel 21:11
"Is not this David the king of the land? Did they not sing to one another of him in dances?"

2 Samuel 6:14
Then David danced and spun around with abandon before Adonai, wearing a linen ritual vest.

Psalm 30:12
You turned my mourning into dancing! You removed my sackcloth and clothed me with joy.

Psalm 87:7
Singers and dancers alike say "For me you are the source of everything."

Psalm 149:3
Let them praise his name with dancing.

Ecclesiastes 3:4
. . . a time to mourn, and a time to dance.

Jeremiah 31:12
"Then the virgin will dance for joy, young men and old men together; for I will turn their mourning into joy, comfort and gladden them after their sorrow."

Luke 15:24–25
For this my son was dead, and is alive again; he was lost, and is found. And they began to celebrate. Now his older son was in the field, and as he came and drew near to the house, he heard music and dancing.

Exulting

*(to rejoice greatly, waving arms wildly and leaping up and down
with extreme joy over our Bridegroom who rejoices over us)*

1 Samuel 2:1
Then Hannah prayed; she said: "My heart exults in Adonai! My dignity has been restored by Adonai! I can gloat over my enemies, because of my joy at your saving me."

Psalm 9:3
I will be glad and exult in you. I will sing praise to your name, 'Elyon.

Psalm 35:9
Then my soul will rejoice in the Lord, exulting in his salvation.

Psalm 63:12
But the king will rejoice in God. Everyone who swears by him will exult, for the mouths of liars will be silenced.

Psalm 64:11
The righteous will rejoice in Adonai; they will take refuge in him; all the upright in heart will exult.

Psalm 68:4
But let the righteous rejoice and be glad in God's presence; yes, let them exult and rejoice.

Psalm 149:5
Let the faithful exult gloriously, let them sing for joy on their beds.

Revelation 19:7
Let us rejoice and exult and give him the glory, for the marriage of the Lamb has come, and his Bride has made herself ready.

BANNERS

(cloth attached to a staff used to announce victory or signify allegiance or a battle standard used to rally the troups; [modern] used to make Adonai's praise glorious)

Exodus 17:15
Moshe built an altar, called it Adonai Nissi [Adonai is my banner/miracle].

Psalm 20:5–6
May he grant you your heart's desire and bring all your plans to success. Then we will shout for joy at your victory and fly our flags in the name of our God.

Song of Solomon 6:4
You are as beautiful as Tirtzah, my love, as lovely as Yerushalayim, but formidable as an army marching under banners.

Isaiah 11:10
On that day the root of Yishai, which stands as a banner for the peoples–the Goyim will seek him out, and the place where he rests will be glorious.

Isaiah 62:10
Go on through, go on through the gates, clear the way for the people! Build up a highway, build it up! Clear away the stones! Raise a banner for the peoples!

Jeremiah 50:2
"Declare it among the nations, proclaim it! Hoist a banner, proclaim it, don't hide it!"

5

ZAMAR

to make music, sing praise or play a musical instrument by plucking or twanging the strings

זָמַד

SHOFARS

(a hollowed out ram's horn used in response to Adonai Tzva'ot's commands
as a signal in war making the enemy tremble; or for celebration of Adonai's victory)

Joshua 6:9
The fighting men went ahead of the cohanim blowing the shofars, while the rearguard marched after the ark, with incessant blowing on the shofars.

Judges 7:22
Gid'on's men blew their 300 shofars, and Adonai caused everyone in the [enemy's] camp to attack his comrades.

2 Samuel 6:15
So David and all the house of Isra'el brought up the ark of Adonai with shouting and the sound of the shofar.

Nehemiah 4:14
"But wherever you are, when you hear the sound of the shofar, come to that place, to us. Our God will fight for us!"

Psalm 47:6
God goes up to shouts of acclaim, Adonai to a blast on the shofar.

Psalm 98:6
With trumpets and the sound of the shofar, shout for joy before the king, Adonai!

Psalm 150:3
Praise him with a blast on the *shofar*!

Joel 2:1
"Blow the shofar in Tziyon! Sound an alarm on my holy mountain!" Let all living in the land tremble, for the Day of Adonai is coming! It's upon us!

Joel 2:15
"Blow the shofar in Tziyon! Proclaim a holy fast, call for a solemn assembly."

(a hammered work of silver used in obedience to our Great High Priest's instructions by his appointed cohanim to sound over an offering, or before going to war)

Numbers 10:8–10

"The trumpets shall be to you for a perpetual statute throughout your generations. And when you go to war in your land against the adversary who oppresses you, then you shall sound an alarm with the trumpets, that you may be remembered before the Lord your God, and you shall be saved from your enemies. Also on your days of rejoicing, at your designated times and on Rosh-Hodesh, you are to sound the trumpets over your burnt offerings and over the sacrifices of your peace offerings; these will be your reminder before your God. I am Adonai your God."

2 Kings 11:14

All the people of the land were celebrating and blowing the trumpets.

1 Chronicles 16:6

B'nayah and Yachzi'el the cohanim blew the trumpets continually before the ark for the covenant of God.

2 Chronicles 7:6

The cohanim stood at their appointed stations, while the L'vi'im used the instruments that David the king had provided for making music to Adonai in order to "give thanks to Adonai, for his grace continues forever," by means of the praises David had composed. Opposite them the cohanim sounded trumpets; and all Isra'el stood up.

2 Chronicles 29:28

The whole assembly prostrated themselves, the singers sang, and the trumpeters sounded; all this continued until the burnt offering was finished.

TAMBOURINES

(a shallow, single-headed hand drum having jingling metal disks in the rim; to be shaken or hit with the knuckles while dancing with great merriment in celebration of our Gracious God)

Exodus 15:20

Also Miryam the prophet, sister of Aharon, took a tambourine in her hand; and all the women went out after her with tambourines, dancing, as Miryam sang to them:

"Sing to Adonai, for he is highly exalted!
The horse and its rider he threw in the sea!"

Psalm 68:24–25

Your procession is seen, O God, the procession of my God, my King, into the sanctuary—the singers in front, the musicians last, in the middle are girls playing tambourines.

Psalm 149:3–4

Let them praise his name with dancing, make melody to him with tambourine and lyre; for Adonai takes delight in his people, he crowns the humble with salvation.

Jeremiah 31:4

Once again, I will build you; you will be rebuilt, virgin of Isra'el. Once again, equipped with your tambourines, you will go out and dance with the merrymakers.

(vibrations are sent out into the atmosphere, pushing back the powers of darkness using a hollow cylinder with membrane stretched tightly over the end or ends, and played by beating with the hands or with sticks)

1 Samuel 18:6

As they were coming home, when David returned from striking down the Philistine, the women came out of all the cities of Israel, singing and dancing, to meet King Saul, with tambourines*, with songs of joy, and with musical instruments.

Job 21:12

They sing to the tambourine (drum) and the lyre and rejoice to the sound of the pipe.

Psalm 81:2

Start the music! Beat the drum! Play the sweet lyre and the lute!

Psalm 149:3

Make music to him with tambourine (drum) and harp.

(Hebrew: *Toph*, also meaning timbrel, tabret, or drum)

CYMBALS

(circular and slightly concave bronze, brass, or wood plates, used with a drumstick, brush, or in pairs struck together producing a crashing sound reminisent of the power of Adonai's voice cracking the cedars)

2 Samuel 6:5

David and the whole house of Isra'el celebrated in the presence of Adonai with all kinds of musical instruments made of cypress-wood, including lyres, lutes, tambourines, rattles and cymbals.

1 Chronicles 15:19

The singers Heman, Asaf and Eitan were appointed to sound the bronze cymbals.

1 Chronicles15:28

So all Isra'el brought up the ark for the covenant of Adonai with shouting; blowing on shofars and trumpets; and cymbals sounding with lutes and lyres.

Ezra 3:10

When the builders laid the foundation of the temple of Adonai, the cohanim in their robes, with trumpets, and the L'vi'im the sons of Asaf, with cymbals, took their places to praise Adonai, as David king of Isra'el had instructed.

Nehemiah 12:27

At the dedication of the wall of Yerushalayim, they sought out the L'vi'im from wherever they had settled to bring them to Yerushalayim and celebrate the dedication with hymns of thanksgiving and with songs accompanied by cymbals, lutes and lyres.

Psalm 150:5

Praise him with clanging cymbals! Praise him with loud crashing cymbals!

(a long slender tube when blown through makes a bright, swirling, whistling timbre that mimics a birdlike sound to the God of All Creation)

1 Samuel 10:5

After that, you will come to Giv'ah of God, where the P'lishtim are garrisoned. On arrival at the city there, you will meet a group of prophets coming down from the high place, preceded by lutes, tambourines, flutes and lyres; and they will be prophesying.

1 Kings 1:40

All the people escorted him back, playing flutes and rejoicing greatly, so that the earth shook with the sound.

Psalm 150:4

Praise him with tambourines and dancing! Praise him with flutes and strings!

LUTES

(a pear shaped instrument with 6 to 13 strings stretched along a neck allowing the player to use harmonics and scales symbolizing God's divine order in sound)

1 Chronicles 13:8

David and all Isra'el celebrated in the presence of God with all their strength, with songs, lyres, lutes, tambourines, cymbals and trumpets.

2 Chronicles 20:28

They came to Yerushalayim with lyres, lutes and trumpets and went to the house of Adonai.

Psalm 57:9

Awake, my glory! Awake, lyre and lute! I will awaken the dawn.

Psalm 71:22

As for me, I will praise you with a lyre for your faithfulness, my God. I will sing praises to you with a lute, Holy One of Isra'el.

Psalm 92:2–4

It is good to give thanks to Adonai and sing praises to your name, 'Elyon, to tell in the morning about your grace and at night about your faithfulness, to the music of a ten-stringed [harp] and a lute, with the melody sounding on a lyre.

Psalm 150:3

Praise him with a blast on the shofar! Praise him with lute and lyre!

Harps

(composed of many strings stretched on a frame of varying sizes and shapes whose resonance when plucked or strummed has a pleasing sound like incense before the throne of God)

Psalm 33:2

Give thanks to Adonai with the lyre, sing praises to you with a ten-stringed harp.

Psalm 92:1–3

It is good to give thanks to Adonai and sing praises to your name, 'Elyon, to tell in the morning about your grace and at night about your faithfulness, to the music of a ten-stringed [harp] and a lute, with the melody sounding on a lyre.

Psalm 144:9

God, I will sing a new song to you; sing praises to him with a ten-stringed harp.

LYRES

(a stringed instrument similar to the harp used to accompany recitations and songs of glory to the One Who Is Worthy)

1 Kings 10:12

The king used the sandalwood to make columns for the house of Adonai and for the royal palace, and also lyres and lutes for the singers. No sandalwood like it has come or been seen to this day.

1 Chronicles 25:3

Of Y'dutun, the descendants of Y'dutun: G'dalyahu, Tzeri, Yesha'yahu, Hashavyahu, Mattityahu—six, with their father Y'dutun, who, accompanied by the lyre, prophesied thanks and praise to Adonai.

Psalm 43:4

Then I will go to the altar of God, to God, my joy and delight; I will praise you on the lyre, God, my God.

Psalm 49:5

I will listen with care to [God's] parable, I will set my enigma to the music of the lyre.

Psalm 98:5

Sing praises to Adonai with the lyre, with the lyre and melodious music!

Psalm 108:3

Awake, lute and lyre! I will awaken the dawn.

Psalm 147:7

Sing to Adonai with thanks, sing praises on the lyre to our God.

(used by the Psalmists these are of various shapes and sizes, with a hollow body and strings stretched on a neck sounded by plucking or pulling a bow across the strings)

1 Samuel 18:6

As David and the others were returning from the slaughter of the P'lishti, the women came out of all the cities of Isra'el to meet King Sha'ul, singing and dancing joyfully with tambourines and three-stringed instruments.

Psalm 6:1

For the leader. With stringed instruments. On sh'minit [low-pitched musical instruments?]. A psalm of David.

Psalm 45:9

Your robes are all fragrant with myrrh, aloes and cassia; from ivory palaces stringed instruments bring you joy.

Isaiah 38:20

"Adonai is ready to save me; hence we will make our stringed instruments sound all the days of our life in the house of Adonai."

Habakkuk 3:19

Elohim Adonai is my strength! He makes me swift and sure-foot as a deer and enables me to stride over my high places. For the leader. With my stringed instruments.

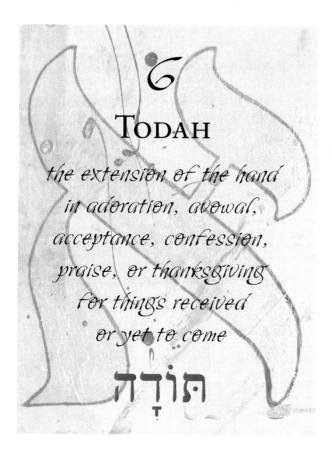

6

TODAH

the extension of the hand
in adoration, avowal,
acceptance, confession,
praise, or thanksgiving
for things received
or yet to come

תּוֹדָה

SACRIFICES

(the act of giving up, destroying, or forgoing something valued to worship Shaddai who supplies all of our needs, even that which is needed to worship him)

Nehemiah 12:43

With joy they offered great sacrifices that day, for God had made them celebrate with great joy. The women and children too rejoiced, so that the celebrating in Yerushalayim could be heard far off.

Psalm 4:6

Offer sacrifices rightly, and put your trust in Adonai.

Psalm 50:23

Whoever offers thanksgiving as his sacrifice honors me.

Psalm 51:19

My sacrifice to God is a broken spirit; God, you won't spurn a broken, chastened heart.

Psalm 54:7–8

May he repay the evil to those who are lying in wait for me. In your faithfulness, destroy them! Then I will generously sacrifice to you; I will praise your name, Adonai, because it is good.

Psalm 107:22

Let them offer sacrifices of thanksgiving and proclaim his great deeds with songs of joy.

Romans 12:1

I exhort you, therefore, brothers, in view of God's mercies, to offer yourselves as a sacrifice, living and set apart for God. This will please him; it is the logical "Temple worship" for you.

1 Peter 2:5

You yourselves, as living stones, are being built into a spiritual house to be cohanim set apart for God to offer spiritual sacrifices acceptable to him through Yeshua the Messiah.

(to make a presentation of something above and beyond the tithe—such as gifts of time, talent, devotion, or money, and dedicating it to Our Provider as a pure gift of praise)

Numbers 10:10

"Also on your days of rejoicing, at your designated times and on Rosh-Hodesh, you are to sound the trumpets over your burnt offerings and over the sacrifices of your peace offerings; these will be your reminder before your God. I am Adonai your God."

Deuteronomy 12:11

Then you will bring all that I am ordering you to the place Adonai your God chooses to have his name live—your burnt offerings, sacrifices, tenths, the offering from your hand, and all your best possessions that you dedicate to Adonai.

Psalm 119:108

Please accept my mouth's voluntary offerings, Adonai; and teach me your rulings.

Hosea 14:3

Take words with you, and return to Adonai; say to him, "Forgive all guilt, and accept what is good; we will pay instead of bulls [the offerings of] our lips."

Malachi 1:11

"For from farthest east to farthest west my name is great among the nations. Offerings are presented to my name everywhere, pure gifts; for my name is great among the nations," says Adonai-Tzva'ot.

Mark 12:33

And to love him with all the heart and with all the understanding and with all the strength, and to love one's neighbor as oneself, is much more than all whole burnt offerings and scarifices.

WAVE OFFERINGS

(to swing, sway, or move to and fro while physically presenting something in worship to the Resurrection and the Life through this action)

Exodus 29:24

And put it all in the hands of Aharon and his sons. They are to wave them as a wave offering in the presence of Adonai.

Leviticus 7:30

He is to bring with his own hands the offerings for Adonai made by fire—he is to bring the breast with its fat. The breast is to be waved as a wave offering before Adonai.

Leviticus 23:11

He is to wave the sheaf before Adonai, so that you will be accepted; the cohen is to wave it on the day after the Shabbat.

Leviticus 23:17

You must bring bread from your homes for waving—two loaves made with one gallon of fine flour, baked with leaven—as firstfruits for Adonai.

Numbers 18:11

"Also yours is the contribution the people of Isra'el give in the form of wave offerings."

(something given to show affection, devotion, gratitude above and beyond all tithes or offerings to give praise to the Lord Who Will See to It)

Ezekiel 20:40

"For on my holy mountain, the high mountain of Isre'el," says Adonai Elohim, "the whole house of Isra'el, all of them, will serve me in the land. I will accept them there, and there I will require your contributions, your best gifts and all your consecrated things."

Malachi 1:11

"For from farthest east to farthest west my name is great among the nations. Offerings are presented to my name everywhere, pure gifts; for my name is great among the nations," says Adonai-Tzva'ot.

Matthew 2:11

Upon entering the house, they saw the child with his mother Miryam; and they prostrated themselves and worshipped him. Then they opened their bags and presented him gifts of gold, frankincense and myrrh.

Luke 6:38

"Give, and you will receive gifts—the full measure, compacted, shaken together and overflowing, will be put right in your lap. For the measure with which you measure out will be used to measure back to you!"

Hebrews 11:4

By trusting, Hevel offered a greater sacrifice than Kayin; because of this, he was attested as righteous, with God giving him this testimony on the ground of his gifts.

BEING A FRAGRANT, SWEET-SMELLING AROMA

(when the fragrance of our life of love and obedience to the Living Bread permeates people and places wherever we go as we live a life of sacrifice that is pleasing to God)

Numbers 28:24

In this fashion you are to offer daily, for seven days, the food of the offering made by fire, making a fragrant aroma for Adonai.

Psalm 147:1

Halleluyah! How good it is to sing praises to our God! How sweet, how fitting to praise him!

Matthew 26:7

A woman who had an alabaster jar filled with very expensive perfume approached Yeshua while he was eating and began pouring it on his head.

John 12:3

Miryam took a whole pint of pure oil of spikenard, which is very expensive, poured it on Yeshua's feet and wiped his feet with her hair, so that the house was filled with the fragrance of the perfume.

Philippians 4:18

I have been more than paid in full: I have been filled, since I have received from Epaphroditus the gifts you sent—they are a fragrant aroma, an acceptable sacrifice, one that pleases God well.

2 Corinthians 2:14–16

But thanks be to God, who . . . through us spreads everywhere the fragrance of what it means to know him! For to God we are the aroma of the Messiah, both among those being saved and among those being lost; to the latter, we are the smell of death leading only to more death; but to the former, we are the sweet smell of life leading to more life. Who is equal to such a task?

KEEPING PURE

(free from sin or guilt, clean, blameless, perfect, faultless, through simple repentance and forgiveness by the blood of Yeshua HaMashiach)

Psalm 24:3–4

Who may go up to the mountain of Adonai? Who can stand in his holy place? Those with clean hands and pure hearts, who don't make vanities the purpose of their lives or swear oaths just to deceive.

Psalm 73:1

How good God is to Isra'el, to those who are pure in heart!

Zephaniah 3:9

For then I will change the peoples, so that they will have pure lips, to call on the name of Adonai, all of them, and serve him with one accord.

Matthew 5:8

"How blessed are the pure in heart! For they will see God."

Philippians 2:14–15

Do everything without *kvetching* [complaining] or arguing, so that you may be blameless and pure children of God, without defect in the midst of a twisted and perverted generation, among whom you shine like stars in the sky.

Hebrews 10:22

Therefore, let us approach the Holiest Place with a sincere heart, in the full assurance that comes from trusting—with out hearts sprinkled clean from a bad conscience and our bodies washed with pure water.

1 John 3:3

And everyone who has this hope in him continues purifying himself, since God is pure.

Repenting

(to be so pained by deep sorrow at the thought of anything breaking relationship or coming between us and the Lover of Our Souls that it leads us to confess our sin)

Isaiah 1:27

Tziyon will be redeemed by justice; and those in her who repent, by righteousness.

Isaiah 55:7

Let the wicked person abandon his way and the evil person his thoughts; let him return to Adonai, and he will have mercy on him; let him return to our God, for he will freely forgive.

Exekiel 18:21

"However, if the wicked person repents of all the sins he committed, keeps my laws and does what is lawful and right; then he will certainly live, he will not die."

Joel 2:13

Tear your heart, not your garments; and turn to Adonai your God. For he is merciful and compassionate, slow to anger, rich in grace, and willing to change his mind about disaster.

Luke 15:10

"In the same way, I tell you, there is joy among God's angels when one sinner repents."

Luke 24:47

And in his name repentance leading to forgiveness of sins is to be proclaimed to people from all nations, starting with Yerushalayim.

Acts 3:19

"Therefore, repent and turn to God, so that your sins may be erased."

Acts 26:20

On the contrary, I announced . . . that they should turn from their sins to God and then do deeds consistent with that repentance.

*(a powerful force of having a peaceful, clean heart free of any negative feelings
or thoughts about another and being in alignment with the word of our Forgiving God)*

Genesis 50:17

Say to Joseph, "Please forgive the transgression of your brothers and their sin, because they did evil to you."

Matthew 6:12, 14–15

Forgive us what we have done wrong, as we too have forgiven those who have wronged us. . . . For if you forgive others their offenses, your heavenly Father will also forgive you; but if you do not forgive others their offenses, your heavenly Father will not forgive yours.

Matthew 18:21

Then Kefa came up and said to him, "Rabbi, how often can my brother sin against me and I have to forgive him? As many as seven times?"

Mark 11:25

"And when you stand praying, if you have anything against anyone, forgive him; so that your Father in heaven may also forgive your offenses."

Luke 17:3

Watch yourselves! If your brother sins, rebuke him; and if he repents, forgive him.

Ephesians 4:32

Instead, be kind to each other, tenderhearted; and forgive each other, just as in the Messiah God has also forgiven you.

Colossians 3:13

Bear with one another; if anyone has a complaint against someone else, forgive him. Indeed, just as the Lord has forgiven you, so you must forgive.

Vows

(a solemn promise or pledge, determined to dedicate oneself before God Who Helps Us to an act, service, or way of life)

Nehemiah 10:28–30

The rest of the people . . . joined their kinsmen and their leaders in swearing an oath, accompanied by a curse [in case of noncompliance], as follows: "We will live by God's Torah, given by Moshe the servant of God, and will perform and obey all the *mitzvot*, rulings and laws of Adonai our Lord."

Psalm 56:13

God, I have made vows to you; I will fulfill them with thank offerings to you.

Psalm 61:6, 9

For you, God, have heard my vows; you have given me the heritage of those who fear your name. . . . Then I will sing praise to your name forever, as day after day I fulfill my vows.

Psalm 65:2

To you, God, in Tziyon, silence is praise; and vows to you are to be fulfilled.

Psalm 76:12

Make vows to Adonai your God, and keep them; all who are around him must bring presents to the one who should be feared.

Isaiah 19:21

They will worship him with sacrifices and offerings, they will make vows to Adonai and keep them.

Matthew 5:33

"Again, you have heard that our fathers were told, 'Do not break your oath,' and 'Keep your vows to Adonai.'"

*(a humble, earnest entreaty, making our supplication or request known
as a petition to the Lord Who Hears, the only one who can help)*

1 Kings 8:28

Even so, Adonai my God, pay attention to your servant's prayer and plea, listen to the cry and prayer that your servant is praying before you today.

1 Kings 9:3

And the Lord said to him, "I have heard your prayer and your plea, which you have made before me."

Psalm 21:3

You give him his heart's desire; you don't refuse the prayer from his lips.

Psalm 66:19

But in fact, God did listen; he paid attention to my prayer.

Matthew 21:22

"In other words, you will receive everything you ask for in prayer, no matter what it is, provided you have trust."

Luke 18:1

Then Yeshua told his talmidim a parable, in order to impress on them that they must always keep praying and not lose heart.

John 14:14

If you ask me for something in my name, I will do it.

Romans 12:12

Rejoice in your hope, be patient in your troubles, and continue steadfastly in prayer.

Philippians 4:6

Don't worry about anything; on the contrary, make your requests known to God by prayer and petition, with thanksgiving.

BEING ONE WITH HIM AND EACH OTHER

*(echad [Hebrew for one]; undivided, of one accord, being one
in spirit and purpose, a complete unity through the Holy Spirit)*

Genesis 5:24

Enoch walked with God, and he was not, for God took him.

Psalm 133:1

Oh, how good, how pleasant it is for brothers to live together in harmony.

John 17:20

"I pray not only for these, but also for those who will trust in me because of their word, that they may all be one. Just as you, Father, are united with me and I with you, I pray that they may be united with us, so that the world may believe that you sent me. The glory which you have given to me, I have given to them; so that they may be one, just as we are one—I united with them and you with me, so that they may be completely one."

Romans 15:6

. . . so that with one accord and with one voice you may glorify the God and Father of our Lord Yeshua the Messiah.

Philippians 1:27–28

Only conduct your lives in a way worthy of the Good News of the Messiah; so that whether I come and see you or I hear about you from a distance, you stand firm, united in spirit, fighting with one accord for the faith of the Good News. Not frightened by anything the opposition does.

Being at Peace with Him and Others

(the absence of quarrels or a calm, quiet, tranquillity while being focused on who God is, the Searcher of All Hearts, and trusting in that truth)

Job 22:21

"Learn to be at peace with [God]; in this way good will come [back] to you."

Isaiah 26:3

You keep him in perfect peace whose mind is stayed on you, because he trusts in you.

Mark 9:50

"Salt is excellent, but if it loses its saltiness, how will you season it? So have salt in yourselves—that is, be at peace with each other."

Luke 2:29–30

"Now, Adonai, according to your word, your servant is at peace as you let him go; for I have seen with my own eyes your *yeshu'ah* [salvation]."

1 Thessalonians 5:13

Treat them with the highest regard and love because of the work they are doing. Live at peace among yourselves.

2 Timothy 2:22

So, flee the passions of youth; and, along with those who call on the Lord from a pure heart, pursue righteousness, faithfulness, love and peace.

1 Peter 3:11

Turn from evil and do good, seek peace and chase after it.

2 Peter 3:14

Therefore, dear friends, as you look for these things, do everything you can to be found by him without spot or defect and at peace.

WALKING VICTORIOUSLY

(success in the contest or struggle against evil involving the overcoming of sin or our enemies and God's and walking the path of the Conqueror)

Deuteronomy 20:4

Because Adonai your God is going with you to fight on your behalf against your enemies and give you victory.

1 Corinthians 9:24–25

Don't you know that in a race all the runners compete, but only one wins the prize? So then, run to win! Now every athlete in training submits himself to strict discipline, and he does it just to win a laurel wreath that will soon wither away. But we do it to win a crown that will last forever.

1 Corinthians 15:57

But thanks be to God, who gives us the victory through our Lord Yeshua the Messiah!

Philippians 3:12–14

It is not that I have already obtained it or already reached the goal—no, I keep pursuing it in the hope of taking hold of that for which the Messiah Yeshua took hold of me. Brothers, I, for my part, do not think of myself as having yet gotten hold of it; but one thing I do: forgetting what is behind me and straining forward toward what lies ahead, I keep pursuing the goal in order to win the prize offered by God's upward calling in the Messiah Yeshua.

Revelation 21:7

He who wins the victory will receive these things, and I will be his God, and he will be my son.

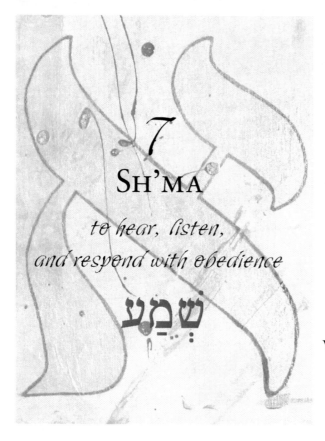

7

SH'MA

to hear, listen,
and respond with obedience

שָׁמַע

LISTENING TO HIM

(hearing with the ears and responding with the heart to the sometimes whispering and sometimes thundering voice of the Spirit of Revelation)

Deuteronomy 6:4

"Sh'ma, Yisra'el! Adonai Eloheinu, Adonai echad [Hear, Isra'el! Adonai our God, Adonai is one]."

Joshua 24:24

The people answered Y'hoshua, "We will serve Adonai our God; we will pay attention to what he says."

Psalm 85:9

I am listening. What will God, Adonai, say?

Psalm 143:8

Make me hear of your love in the morning, because I rely on you. Make me know the way I should walk, because I entrust myself to you.

Ezekiel 40:4

The man said to me, "Human being, look with your eyes, hear with your ears, and pay attention to all the things I am showing you; because the reason you were brought here is so that I could show them to you. Tell everything you see to the house of Isra'el."

Matthew 17:5

While he was still speaking, a bright cloud enveloped them; and a voice from the cloud said, "This is my Son, whom I love, with whom I am well pleased. Listen to him!"

John 10:3

This is the one the gate-keeper admits, and the sheep hear his voice. He calls his own sheep, each one by name, and leads them out.

Revelation 2:7

"Those who have ears, let them hear what the Spirit is saying to the Messianic communities."

(a firm faith or confidence in the honesty, integrity, and reliability of the God Who Carries You, with assured expectation and anticipation in his trustworthiness)

Psalm 4:6
Offer sacrifices rightly, and put your trust in Adonai.

Psalm 26:1
Vindicate me, Adonai, for I have lived a blameless life; unwaveringly I trust in Adonai.

Psalm 31:7
I hate those who serve worthless idols; as for me, I trust in Adonai.

Psalm 37:3
Trust in Adonai, and do good; settle in the land, and feed on faithfulness.

Psalm 56:3–4
When I am afraid, I put my trust in you.
In God—I praise his word—in God I trust;
I have no fear; what can human power do to me?

Psalm 115:11
You who fear Adonai, trust in Adonai! He is their help and shield.

Proverbs 3:5
Trust in Adonai with all your heart; do not rely on your own understanding.

Isaiah 26:4
Trust in Adonai forever, because in Yah Adonai is a Rock of Ages.

Isaiah 50:10
Who among you fears Adonai? Who obeys what his servant says? Even when he walks in the dark, without any light, he will trust in Adonai's reputation and rely on his God.

Hebrews 2:13
And again, "I will put my trust in him."

Following Him

(step by step to chase devotedly, dogedly pursue, go after or go along with our Faithful Shepherd fully focusing all your attention on him and his way)

1 Samuel 12:20

Sh'mu'el answered the people, "Don't be afraid. you have indeed done all this evil; yet now, just don't turn away from following Adonai; but serve Adonai with all your heart."

2 Kings 23:3

The king stood on the platform and made a covenant in the presence of Adonai to live following Adonai. . .

2 Chronicles 34:33

Yoshiyahu removed all the abominable idols from all the territories belonging to the people of Isra'el, and he made everyone in Isra'el serve Adonai their God. Throughout his lifetime, they did not stop following Adonai, the God of their ancestors.

Matthew 19:21

Yeshua said to him, "If you are serious about reaching the goal, go and sell your possessions, give to the poor, and you will have riches in heaven. Then come, follow me!"

Mark 1:17–18

Yeshua said to them, "Come, follow me, and I will make you into fishers for men!" At once they left their nets and followed him.

John 10:4, 27–28

After taking out all that are his own, he goes on ahead of them; and the sheep follow him because they recognize his voice. . . . My sheep listen to my voice, I recognize them, they follow me, and I give them eternal life.

TRUSTING HIS PROMISES

(an undying belief that God Who Knows Everything will keep his word no matter how things look at the moment)

Numbers 23:19

"God is not a human who lies or a mortal who changes his mind. When he says something, he will do it; when he makes a promise, he will fulfill it."

1 Kings 8:56

"Blessed be Adonai, who has given rest to his people Isra'el, in accordance with everything he promised. Not one word has failed of his good promise, which he made through Moshe his servant."

Psalm 60:8

God in his holiness spoke, and I took joy [in his promise].

Psalm 119:103

How sweet to my tongue is your promise, truly sweeter than honey in my mouth!

Psalm 119:162

I take joy in your promise, like someone who finds much booty.

Luke 1:45

"Indeed you are blessed, because you have trusted that the promise Adonai has made to you will be fulfilled."

Hebrews 10:23

Let us continue holding fast to the hope we acknowledge, without wavering; for the One who made the promise is trustworthy.

2 Peter 3:9

The Lord is not slow in keeping his promise, as some people think of slowness; on the contrary, he is patient with you; for it is not his purpose that anyone should be destroyed, but that everyone should turn from his sins.

Having Faith in Him

(unquestioning belief in our Rock that does not require proof, evidence, or resolution; having an unexplainable certainty in him)

Isaiah 7:9
Without firm faith, you will not be firmly established.

1 Corinthians 16:13
Stay alert, stand firm in the faith, behave like a *mentsh* [good, moral person], grow strong.

1 Timothy 6:12
Fight the good fight of the faith, take hold of the eternal life to which you were called when you testified so well to your faith before many witnesses.

2 Timothy 4:7
I have fought the good fight, I have finished the race, I have kept the faith.

James 2:1
My brothers, practice the faith of our Lord Yeshua, the glorious Messiah, without showing favoritism.

James 2:5
Listen, my dear brothers, hasn't God chosen the poor of the world to be rich in faith and to receive the Kingdom which he promised to those who love him?

James 2:23
. . . and the passage of the Tanakh was fulfilled which says, "Avraham had faith in God, and it was credited to his account as righteousness." He was even called God's friend.

Jude 1:20
But you, dear friends, build yourselves up in your most holy faith, and pray in union with the Ruach HaKodesh.

Obeying His Word

(to precisely carry out, be guided by, or submit to the authority and wisdom of the powerful double-edged Sword of the Lord)

Exodus 24:3

Moshe came and told the people everything Adonai had said, including all the rulings. The people answered with one voice: "We will obey every word Adonai has spoken."

Leviticus 18:4

You are to obey my rulings and laws and live accordingly; I am Adonai your God.

Deuteronomy 32:46–47

"Take to heart all the words of my testimony against you today, so that you can use them in charging your children to be careful to obey all the words of this Torah. For this is not a trivial matter for you; on the contrary, it is your life!"

Psalm 119:112

I have resolved to obey your laws forever, at every step.

Proverbs 7:2

Obey my commands, and live; guard my teaching like the pupil of your eye.

Luke 11:28

But he said, "Far more blessed are those who hear the word of God and obey it!"

1 John 3:24

Those who obey his commands remain united with him and he with them. Here is how we know that he remains united with us: by the Spirit who he gave us.

Revelation 3:3

So remember what you received and heard, and obey it, and turn from your sin! For if you don't wake up, I will come like a thief; and you don't know at what moment I will come upon you.

Paying Attention to Him

*(to keep one's mind focused closely on our Wonder of
a Counselor, with true devotion or pure concentration)*

Exodus 15:26

He said, "If you will listen intently to the voice
of Adonai your God, do what he considers
right, pay attention to his *mitzvot* and observe
his laws, I will not afflict you with any of the
diseases I brought on the Egyptians; because I
am Adonai your healer."

Exodus 23:13

Pay attention to everything I have said to you;
do not invoke the names of other gods or even
let them be heard crossing your lips.

Deuteronomy 12:28

Obey and pay attention to everything I am
ordering you to do, so that things will go well
with you and with your descendants after you
forever. As you do what Adonai sees as good
and right.

Joshua 24:24

The people answered Y'hoshua, "We will serve
Adonai our God; we will pay attention to what
he says."

Isaiah 51:4

"Pay attention to me, my people! My nation,
listen to me! For Torah will go out from me; I
will claim them with my justice as a light for
the peoples."

Mark 4:24

And he [Yeshua] said to them, "Pay attention
to what you hear."

Hebrews 2:1

Therefore we must pay much closer attention to
what we have heard, lest we drift away from it.

OBSERVING HIS WAYS

(to take notice or pay special attention to Yeshua's life, and to watch over, guard, follow, keep, or celebrate the Giver of Torah's instructions)

Leviticus 20:8

Observe my regulations, and obey them; I am Adonai, who sets you apart to be holy.

Numbers 9:2

Let the people of Isra'el observe *Pesach* at its designated time.

Deuteronomy 26:18

In turn Adonai is agreeing today that you are his own unique treasure, as he promised you; that you are to observe all his *mitzvot*.

Psalm 119:2

How happy are those who observe his instruction, who seek him wholeheartedly!

Psalm 119:55

I remember your name, Adonai, at night; and I observe your Torah.

Isaiah 41:20

Then the people will see and know, together observe and understand that the hand of Adonai has done this, that the Holy One of Isra'el created it.

Revelation 14:12

This is when perseverance is needed on the part of God's people, those who observe his commands and exercise Yeshua's faithfulness.

WALKING IN HIS PRESENCE

(to be closely connected to, obedient to, aware of and focused on the Light of the World and to be filled with and reflect this light)

Genesis 17:1

When Avram was 99 years old Adonai appeared to Avram and said to him, "I am El Shaddai [God Almighty]. Walk in my presence and be pure-hearted."

1 Samuel 2:30

"Therefore Adonai the God of Isra'el says, 'I did indeed say that your family and your father's family would walk in my presence forever.'"

1 Kings 8:25

Now therefore, Adonai, God of Isra'el, keep what you promised to your servant David, my father, when you said, "You will never lack a man in my presence to sit on the throne of Isra'el, if only your children are careful about what they do, so that they live in my presence, just as you have lived in my presence."

Acts 2:28

You have made known to me the ways of life; you will fill me with joy by your presence.

Acts 3:19–20

Therefore, repent and turn to God, so that your sins may be erased; so that times of refreshing may come from the Lord's presence.

1 John 5:14

This is the confidence we have in his presence: if we ask anything that accords with his will, he hears us.

REMEMBERING HIS COVENANT

(to observe, celebrate, or maintain a promise, and not to forget our legal/ spiritual, blood-cut, eternal agreement with the Ancient of Days)

Genesis 17:7

"I am establishing my covenant between me and you, along with your descendants after you, generation after generation, as an everlasting covenant, to be God for you and for your descendants after you."

Exodus 9:5

Now if you will pay careful attention to what I say and keep my covenant, then you will be my own treasure from among all the peoples, for all the earth is mine.

Exodus 24:7

Then he took the book of the covenant and read it aloud, so that the people could hear; and they responded, "Everything that Adonai has spoken, we will do and obey."

Exodus 31:16

The people of Isra'el are to keep the Shabbat, to observe Shabbat through all their generations as a perpetual covenant.

Exodus 34:28

Moshe was there with Adonai forty days and forty nights, during which time he neither ate food nor drank water. [Adonai] wrote on the tablets the words of the covenant, the Ten Words.

Matthew 26:28

For this is my blood, which ratifies the New Covenant, my blood shed on behalf of many, so that they may have their sins forgiven.

Hebrews 10:16

"'This is the covenant which I will make with them after those days.' says Adonai: 'I will put my Torah on their hearts, and write it on their minds.'"

MEDITATING ON HIM AND HIS WORD

*(to reflect on, study, ponder, think deeply and continuously on all
that is him and all that the True and Faithful Witness says)*

Joshua 1:8
Yes, keep this book of the Torah on your lips, and meditate on it day and night, so that you will take care to act according to everything written in it. Then your undertakings will prosper, and you will succeed.

Psalm 1:2
Their delight is in Adonai's Torah; on his Torah they meditate day and night.

Psalm 63:6–7
I am as satisfied as with rich food; my mouth praises you with joy on my lips when I remember you on my bed and meditate on you in the night watches.

Psalm 77:13
I will meditate on your work and think about what you have done.

Psalm 119:15
I will meditate on your precepts and keep my eyes on your ways.

Psalm 119:27
Make me understand the way of your precepts, and I will meditate on your wonders.

Psalm 119:78
Let the proud be ashamed, because they wrong me with lies; as for me, I will meditate on your precepts.

Psalm 119:97, 99
How I love your Torah! I meditate on it all day. . . . I have more understanding than all my teachers, because I meditate on your instruction.

Luke 2:19
But Mary treasured up all these things, pondering them in her heart.

(listening to the voice of the Lord Who Has Anointed Me through dreams and their interpretation, words of knowledge, visions, and the written Word)

Genesis 41:11–12

One night both I and he had dreams, and each man's dream had its own meaning. There was with us a young man, a Hebrew, a servant of the captain of the guard; and we told him our dreams, and he interpreted them for us—he interpreted each man's dream individually.

Deuteronomy 33:3–4

He truly loves the people—all his holy ones are in your hand; sitting at your feet they receive your instruction, the *Torah* Moshe commanded us as an inheritance for the community of Ya'akov.

2 Chronicles 26:5

He consulted God during the lifetime of Z'kharyahu, who understood visions of God; and as long as he consulted Adonai, God gave him success.

1 Corinthians 12:8

To one, through the Spirit, I give a word of wisdom; to another, a word of knowledge, in accordance with the same Spirit.

1 Corinthians 14:26

What is our conclusion, brothers? Whenever you come together, let everyone be ready with a psalm or a teaching or a revelation, or ready to use his gift of tongues or give an interpretation; but let everything be for edification.

Galatians 1:12

. . . because neither did I receive it from someone else nor was I taught it—it came through a direct revelation from Yeshua the Messiah.

Working Miracles or Healings

(Holy Spirit empowered unexplainable happenings that contradict known scientific laws, recovery or wholeness brought about supernaturally; acts of God)

Exodus 7:9
"When Pharaoh says to you, 'Perform a miracle,' tell Aharon to take his staff and throw it down in front of Pharaoh, so that it can become a snake."

Proverbs 12:18
The tongue of the wise brings healing.

Luke 9:6
They set out and went through village after village, healing and announcing the Good News everywhere.

Acts 3:16
And it is through putting trust in his name that his name has given strength to this man whom you see and know. Yes, it is the trust that comes through Yeshua which has given him this perfect healing in the presence of you all.

Acts 4:30
"Stretch out your hand to heal and to do signs and miracles through the name of your holy servant Yeshua!"

Acts 5:12
Meanwhile, through the emissaries many signs and miracles continued to be done among the people.

Acts 7:36
This man led them out, performing miracles and signs in Egypt, at the Red Sea and in the wilderness for forty years.

1 Corinthians 12:28
And God has placed in the Messianic Community first, emissaries; second, prophets; third, teachers; then those who work miracles; then those with gifts of healing . . .

Walking in His Authority

(spiritual legal power or right to take action as his emissaries on behalf of the Most High King, as if we bear his signet ring)

Isaiah 22:22

And I will place on his shoulder the key of the house of David. He shall open, and none shall shut; and he shall shut, and none shall open.

Matthew 9:8

When the crowds saw this, they were awestruck and said a b'rakhah to God the Giver of such authority to human beings.

Matthew 10:1

Yeshua called his twelve talmidim and gave them authority to drive out unclean spirits and to heal every kind of disease and weakness.

Matthew 16:19

I will give you the keys of the Kingdom of Heaven. Whatever you prohibit on earth will be prohibited in heaven, and whatever you permit on earth will be permitted in heaven.

Luke 9:1–2

Calling together the Twelve, Yeshua gave them power and authority to expel all the demons and to cure diseases; and he sent them out to proclaim the Kingdom of God and to heal.

Luke 10:19

Remember, I have given you authority; so you can trample down snakes and scorpions, indeed, all the Enemy's forces; and you will remain completely unharmed.

Titus 2:15

These are the things you should say. Encourage and rebuke with full authority; don't let anyone look down on you.

WARRING IN THE SPIRIT

(combating God's enemies in spiritual ways and being armed and dangerous with our Warrior's spiritual weapons and strategies; his battle-axe)

2 Samuel 22:35, 38, 40
He trains my hands for war until my arms can bend a bow of bronze. . . . I pursued my enemies and wiped them out, without turning back until they were destroyed. . . . For you braced me with strength for the battle and bent down my adversaries beneath me.

Isaiah 13:4
Adonai-Tzva'ot is mustering an army for war.

2 Corinthians 10:3–5
For although we do live in the world, we do not wage war in a worldly way; because the weapons we use to wage war are not worldly. On the contrary, they have God's power for demolishing strongholds.

Ephesians 6:13–17
So take up every piece of war equipment God provides; so that when the evil day comes, you will be able to resist; and when the battle is won, you will still be standing. Therefore, stand! Have the belt of truth buckled around your waist, put on righteousness for a breastplate, and wear on your feet the readiness that comes from the Good News of shalom. Always carry the shield of trust, with which you will be able to extinguish all the flaming arrows of the Evil One. And take the helmet of deliverance; along with the word given by the Spirit, that is, the Word of God.

Philippians 1:29–30
And this is from God; because for the Messiah's sake it has been granted to you not only to trust in him but also to suffer on his behalf, to fight the same battles you once saw me fight and now hear that I am still fighting.

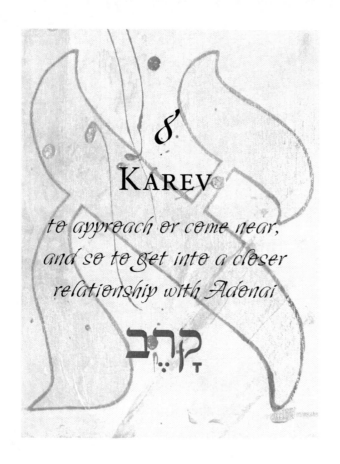

8

KAREV

*to approach or come near,
and so to get into a closer
relationship with Adonai*

קָרֵב

SERVING HIM

*(giving of ourselves to Adonai and others, in obedient devotion
and out of love for Him Who Takes Delight in Us)*

Deuternomony 10:12

So now, Isra'el, all that Adonai your God asks
from you is to fear Adonai your God, follow all
his ways, love him and serve Adonai your God
with all your heart and all your being.

1 Samuel 12:20

Sh'mu'el answered the people, "Don't be
afraid. You have indeed done all this evil; yet
now, just don't turn away from following Adonai; but serve Adonai with all your heart."

Psalm 100:2

Serve Adonai with gladness. Enter his presence
with joyful songs.

Malachi 3:18

Then once again you will see the difference between the righteous and the wicked, between
the person who serves God and one that doesn't
serve him.

Luke 22:27

For who is greater? The one reclining at the
table? or the one who serves? It's the one reclining at the table, isn't it? But I myself am among
you like one who serves.

John 12:26

If someone is serving me, let him follow me;
wherever I am, my servant will be there too.
My Father will honor anyone who serves me.

Colossians 3:23

Whatever work you do, put yourself into it, as
those who are serving not merely other people,
but the Lord.

(desire accompanied by peaceful expectation that our God of Love will hear our prayers and confidently believing he is able to do more than we can ask or imagine)

Psalm 27:14

Put your hope in Adonai, be strong, and let your heart take courage! Yes, put your hope in Adonai!

Psalm 37:34

Put your hope in Adonai, keep to his way, and he will raise you up to inherit the land.

Isaiah 40:30–31

Young men may grow tired and weary, even the fittest may stumble and fall; but those who hope in Adonai will renew their strength, they will soar aloft as with eagles' wings; when they are running they won't grow weary, when they are walking they won't get tired.

Romans 4:18

In hope he [Abraham] believed against hope, that he should become the father of many nations.

1 Corinthians 13:7

Love always bears up, always trusts, always hopes, always endures.

1 Timothy 6:17

As for those who do have riches in this present world, charge them not to be proud and not to let their hopes rest on the uncertainties of riches but to rest their hopes on God, who richly provides us with all things for our enjoyment.

1 Peter 1:13

Therefore, get your minds ready for work, keep yourselves under control, and fix your hopes fully on the gift you will receive when Yeshua the Messiah is revealed.

DOING GOOD

(doing what is effective or efficient, beneficial or honorable, respectable or kind, or whatever is virtuous in the eyes of the God of Goodness)

Exodus 33:19

And he said, "I will make all my goodness pass before you and will proclaim before you my name 'The Lord.'

Psalm 34:15

Turn from evil, and do good; seek peace, go after it!

Psalm 37:3

Trust in Adonai, and do good; settle in the land, and feed on faithfulness.

Psalm 37:27

If you turn from evil and do good, you will live safely forever.

Isaiah 1:17

Learn to do good! Seek justice, relieve the oppressed, defend orphans, plead for the widow.

Luke 6:33

What credit is it to you if you do good only to those who do good to you? Even sinners do that. . . . But love your enemies, do good, and lend expecting nothing back! Your reward will be great, and you will be children of Ha'Elyon.

1 Timothy 6:18

Charge them to do good, to be rich in good deeds, to be generous and ready to share.

Titus 2:14

He gave himself up on our behalf in order to free us from all violation of Torah and purify for himself a people who would be his own, eager to do good.

(selfless acts of kindness, and good deeds toward those nearest us and treating our neighbor as we want to be treated in obedience to Yeshua's greatest commandment)

Leviticus 19:18

Don't take vengeance on or bear a grudge against any of your people; rather, love your neighbor as yourself; I am Adonai.

Proverbs 17:17

A friend loves at all times.

Matthew 5:43–44

"You have heard that our fathers were told, 'Love your neighbor—and hate your enemy.' But I tell you, love your enemies! Pray for those who persecute you!"

Matthew 19:19

Honor father and mother and love your neighbor as yourself.

Mark 12:31

"The second is this: 'You are to love your neighbor as yourself.' There is no other *mitzvah* greater than these."

John 13:34

I am giving you a new command: that you keep on loving each other. In the same way that I have loved you, you are also to keep on loving each other.

Romans 13:9

For the commandments, "Don't commit adultery," "Don't murder," "Don't steal," "Don't covet," and any others are summed up in this one rule: "Love your neighbor as yourself."

BEING HOLY

(cleansed from sin, consecrated, sacred, pure according to God's standards and being sound and whole through the Spotless Lamb's blood)

Leviticus 11:44

For I am Adonai your God; therefore, consecrate yourselves and be holy, for I am holy.

Leviticus 20:26

Rather, you people are to be holy for me; because I, Adonai, am holy; and I have set you apart from the other peoples, so that you can belong to me.

Ephesians 1:4

In the Messiah he chose us in love before the creation of the universe to be holy and without defect in his presence.

Ephesians 4:23

Clothe yourselves with the new nature created to be godly, which expresses itself in the righteousness and holiness that flow from the truth.

Hebrews 10:14

For by a single offering he has brought to the goal for all time those who are being set apart for God and made holy.

Hebrews 12:14

Keep pursuing shalom with everyone and the holiness without which no one will see the Lord.

1 Peter 1:15–16

On the contrary, following the Holy One who called you, become holy yourselves in your entire way of life; since the Tanakh says, "You are to be holy because I am holy."

Putting on Righteous Garments

(cleansing ourselves through confession and repentance so we can stand before the God Who Formed Us in the Womb clothed in the purity of his Son)

Exodus 39:1

From the blue, purple, and scarlet yarn they made the garments for officiating, for serving in the Holy Place; and they made the holy garments for Aharon, as Adonai had ordered Moshe.

Zechariah 3:3–4

Y'hoshua was clothed in garments covered with dung; and he was standing before the angel, who said to those standing in front of him, "Take those filthy garments off of him." Then to him he said, "See, I am taking your guilt away. I will clothe you in fine robes."

Revelation 3:5

He who wins the victory will, like them, be dressed in white clothing; and I will not blot his name out of the Book of Life; in fact, I will acknowledge him individually before my Father and before his angels.

Revelation 7:14

Then he told me, "These are the people who have come out of the Great Persecution. They have washed their robes and made them white with the blood of the Lamb."

Revelation 16:15

"Look! I am coming like a thief! How blessed are those who stay alert and keep their clothes clean, so that they won't be walking naked and be publicly put to shame!"

Revelation 22:14

How blessed are those who wash their robes, so that they have the right to eat from the Tree of Life and go through the gates into the city!

BEING SET APART

*(separated, prepared, bought with a price, and reserved only
for our Very Great Reward and his purposes)*

Deuteronomy 7:6

For you are a people set apart as holy for
Adonai your God. Adonai your God has
chosen you out of all the peoples on the face of
the earth to be his own unique treasure.

Deuteronomy 28:9

Adonai will establish you as a people separated
out for himself, as he has sworn to you—if you
will observe the *mitzvot* of Adonai your God
and follow his ways.

Jeremiah 1:5

"Before I formed you in the womb, I knew you;
before you were born, I separated you for myself. I have appointed you to be a prophet to the
nations."

John 17:17, 19

Set them apart for holiness by means of the
truth—your word is truth. . . . On their behalf
I am setting myself apart for holiness, so that
they too may be set apart for holiness by means
of the truth.

Hebrews 10:10

It is in connection with this will that we have
been separated for God and made holy, once
and for all, through the offering of Yeshua the
Messiah's body.

1 Peter 2:5

You yourselves, as living stones, are being built
into a spiritual house to be cohanim set apart
for God to offer spiritual sacrifices acceptable
to him through Yeshua the Messiah.

(a complete yielding to the Ruach HaKodesh or Breath of God, to be equipped and empowered to obey God's word and filled with his fruit and gifts)

Genesis 41:38

Pharaoh said to his officials, "Can we find anyone else like him? The Spirit of God lives in him!"

Ezekiel 39:29

"And I will not hide my face anymore from them, when I pour out my Spirit upon the house of Israel," declares the Lord God.

Joel 2:28

And it shall come to pass afterward, that I will pour out my Spirit on all flesh.

John 20:22

Having said this, he breathed on them and said to them, "Receive the Ruach HaKodesh!"

Romans 8:5–6

For those who identify with their old nature set their minds on the things of the old nature, but those who identify with the Spirit set their minds on the things of the Spirit. Having one's mind controlled by the old nature is death, but having one's mind controlled by the Spirit is life and shalom.

1 Corinthians 3:16

Don't you know that you people are God's temple and that God's Spirit lives in you?

1 Corinthians 10:3

Also they all ate the same food from the Spirit, and they all drank the same drink from the Spirit—for they drank from a Spirit-sent Rock which followed them, and that Rock was the Messiah.

Philippians 4:13

I can do all things through him who gives me power.

WAITING ON HIM

*(being calm, focused, patient and expectantly trusting as we look
to our Advocate for the future and surrender our own agenda)*

Psalm 5:4

Adonai, in the morning you will hear my voice;
in the morning I lay my needs before you and
wait expectantly.

Psalm 25:3

No one waiting for you will be disgraced; disgrace awaits those who break faith for no reason.

Psalm 130:5–6

I wait longingly for Adonai; I put my hope in
his word. Everything in me waits for Adonai
more than guards on watch wait for morning,
more than guards on watch wait for morning.

Isaiah 25:9

On that day they will say, "See! This is our God!
We waited for him to save us. This is Adonai; we
put our hope in him. We are full of joy, so glad
he saved us!"

Lamentations 3:25–26

Adonai is good to those waiting for him, to
those who are seeking him out. It is good to
wait patiently for the saving help of Adonai.

Micah 7:7

But as for me, I will look to Adonai, I will wait
for the God of my salvation; my God will hear
me.

Romans 8:22–23

We know that until now, the whole creation has
been groaning as with the pains of childbirth;
and not only it, but we ourselves, who have the
firstfruits of the Spirit, groan inwardly as we
continue waiting eagerly to be made sons—that
is, to have our whole bodies redeemed and set
free.

ENDURING

(to bear, last, continue on, or remain, and to hold up under pain, fatigue, temptation, spiritual warfare, or persecution for the Kingdom of God)

Exodus 18:19–23

"So listen now to what I have to say. I will give you some advice, and God will be with you. . . . If you do this—and God is directing you to do it— you will be able to endure; and all these people too will arrive at their destination peacefully."

1 Corinthians 10:13

No temptation has seized you beyond what people normally experience, and God can be trusted not to allow you to be tempted beyond what you can bear. On the contrary, along with the temptation he will also provide the way out, so that you will be able to endure.

2 Corinthians 1:6

So if we undergo trials, it is for your encouragement and deliverance; and if we are encouraged, that should encourage you when you have to endure sufferings like those we are experiencing.

2 Timothy 4:5

But you, remain steady in every situation, endure suffering, do the work that a proclaimer of the Good News should, and do everything your service to God requires.

Hebrews 12:1–2

So then, since we are surrounded by such a great cloud of witnesses, let us, too, put aside every impediment—that is, the sin which easily hampers our forward movement—and keep running with endurance in the contest set before us, looking away to the Initiator and Completer of that trusting, Yeshua—who, in exchange for obtaining the joy set before him, endured execution on a stake as a criminal, scorning the shame, and has sat down at the right hand of the throne of God.

SUFFERING

*(to endure pain, harm, injury, loss, or evil to receive an eternal inheritance
of much greater value; to suffer as Yeshua suffered for us)*

Nehemiah 9:32

"Now therefore, our God, great, mighty, fear-some God, who keeps both covenant and grace: let not all this suffering seem little to you that has come on us, our kings, our leaders, our cohanim, our prophets, our ancestors, and on all your people, from the times of the kings of Ashur until this very day."

Psalm 37:18

Adonai knows what the wholehearted suffer, but their inheritance lasts forever.

Psalm 90:15

Let our joy last as long as the time you made us suffer, for as many years as we experienced trouble.

Romans 8:17

And if we are children, then we are also heirs, heirs of God and joint-heirs with the Messiah—provided we are suffering with him in order also to be glorified with him.

1 Corinthians 12:26

Thus if one part suffers, all the parts suffer with it; and if one part is honored, all the parts share its happiness.

2 Timothy 1:8

So don't be ashamed of bearing testimony to our Lord or to me, his prisoner. On the contrary, accept your share in suffering disgrace for the sake of the Good News. God will give you the strength for it.

1 Peter 3:14

But even if you do suffer for being righteous, you are blessed! Moreover, don't fear what they fear or be disturbed.

PERSEVERING

*(to continue on in spite of difficulty, opposition, or testing and
to be steadfast for the sake of the God Who Sees and who will sustain us)*

Genesis 7:23

Only Noah was left, and those who were with him in the ark. And the waters prevailed on the earth 150 days.

Genesis 18:13, 21:5

The Lord said to Abraham, "Why did Sarah laugh and say, 'Shall I indeed bear a child, now that
I am old?' Is anything too hard for the Lord?" . . . Abraham was a hundred years old when his son Isaac was born to him.

Romans 8:25

But if we continue hoping for something we don't see, then we still wait eagerly for it, with perseverance.

1 Thessalonians 1:3

Calling to mind before God our Father what our Lord Yeshua the Messiah has brought about in you—how your trust produces action, your love hard work, and your hope perseverance.

2 Thessalonians 3:5

May the Lord direct your hearts into God's love and the perseverance which the Messiah gives.

James 1:3–4

For you know that the testing of your trust produces perseverance. But let perseverance do its complete work; so that you may be complete and whole, lacking in nothing.

Revelation 2:3

You are persevering, and you have suffered for my sake without growing weary.

Fasting

(to abstain from all or certain foods as a sacrifice to subdue the flesh and strengthen the spirit, sometimes done in preparation for ministry or prayer, or on Holy Days; to humble yourself before the Face of God)

Esther 4:16

Go assemble all the Jews to be found in Shushan, and have them fast for me, neither eating nor drinking for three days, night and day; also I and the girls attending me will fast the same way.

Isaiah 58:6–7

"Here is the sort of fast I want—releasing those unjustly bound, untying the thongs of the yoke, letting the oppressed go free, breaking every yoke, sharing your food with the hungry, taking the homeless poor into your house, clothing the naked when you see them, fulfilling your duty to your kinsmen!"

Daniel 9:3

I turned to Adonai, God, to seek an answer, pleading with him in prayer, with fasting, sackcloth and ashes.

Joel 2:12

"Yet even now," says Adonai, "turn to me with all your heart, with fasting, weeping and lamenting."

Matthew 6:16–18

"Now when you fast, don't go around looking miserable, like the hypocrites. They make sour faces so that people will know they are fasting. Yes! I tell you, they have their reward already! But you, when you fast, wash your face and groom yourself, so that no one will know you are fasting—except your Father, who is with you in secret. Your Father, who sees what is done in secret, will reward you."

Acts 13:3

After fasting and praying, they placed their hands on them and sent them off.

*(to make a loud vocal sound, to sob and shed tears, to plead
from our hearts to the One Who is Our Comforter)*

Psalm 88:2–3

Adonai, God of my salvation, when I cry out to you in the night, let my prayer come before you, turn your ear to my cry for help!

Psalm 88:14

But I cry out to you, Adonai; my prayer comes before you in the morning.

Lamentations 2:19

Get up! Cry out in the night, at the beginning of every watch! Pour your heart out like water before the face of Adonai!

Joel 1:14

Proclaim a holy fast, call for a solemn assembly, gather the leaders and all who live in the land to the house of Adonai your God, and cry out to Adonai.

Jonah 3:8–9

They must be covered with sackcloth, both people and animals; and they are to cry out to God with all their might—let each of them turn from his evil way and from the violence they practice. Who knows? Maybe God will change his mind, relent and turn from his fierce anger; and then we won't perish.

Romans 8:15

For you did not receive a spirit of slavery to bring you back again into fear; on the contrary, you received the Spirit, who makes us sons and by whose power we cry out, "Abba!" (that is, "Dear Father!")

Passing the Test

(going through extreme or unusual momentary trials to be purified, strengthened and pruned to grow stronger under the watchful eye of the Gardener)

Job 23:10
Yet he knows the way I take; when he has tested me, I will come out like gold.

Isaiah 48:10
"Look, I have refined you, but not [as severely] as silver; [rather] I have tested you in the furnace of affliction."

Zechariah 13:9
"That third part I will bring through the fire; I will refine them as silver is refined, I will test them as gold is tested. They will call on my name, and I will answer them. I will say, 'This is my people' and they will say, 'Adonai is my God.'"

John 15:1–3, 8
"I am the real vine, and my Father is the gardener. Every branch which is part of me but fails to bear fruit, he cuts off; and every branch that does bear fruit, he prunes, so that it may bear more fruit. Right now, because of the word which I have spoken to you, you are pruned. . . . This is how my Father is glorified—in your bearing much fruit; this is how you will prove to be my *talmidim.*"

1 Thessalonians 2:4
Instead, since God has tested us and found us fit to be entrusted with Good News, this is how we speak: not to win favor with people but with God, who tests our hearts.

1 Peter 1:7
Even gold is tested for genuineness by fire. The purpose of these trials is so that your trust's genuineness, which is far more valuable than perishable gold, will be judged worthy of praise, glory and honor at the revealing of Yeshua the Messiah.

9

SHABACH

*to exclaim, shout,
and triumph
in a loud tone or to give
glory, laud, or praise;
to commend*

שָׁבַח

PROCLAIMING HIS PRAISES

*(to announce officially, cry out, praise or extol from the heart
our Righteous One's gracious, mighty doings)*

Psalm 40:6

How much you have done, Adonai my God!
Your wonders and your thoughts toward us—
none can compare with you! I would proclaim
them, I would speak about them; but there's too
much to tell!

Psalm 71:18–19, 24

So now that I'm old, and my hair is gray, don't
abandon me, God, till I have proclaimed your
strength to the next generation, your power to
all who will come, your righteousness too, God,
which reaches to the heights. . . . All day long my
tongue will speak of your righteousness.

Psalm 89:2

I will sing about Adonai's acts of grace forever,
with my mouth proclaim your faithfulness to
all generations.

Psalm 92:15–16

Even in old age they will be vigorous, still full
of sap, still bearing fruit, proclaiming that
Adonai is upright, my Rock, in whom there is
no wrong.

Psalm 106:2

Who can express Adonai's mighty doings or
proclaim in full his praise?

Psalm 145:7

They will gush forth the fame of your abound-
ing goodness, and they will sing of your
righteousness.

Luke 8:39

"Return to your home, and declare how much
God has done for you." And he went away, pro-
claiming throughout the whole city how much
Yeshua had done for him.

SHOUTING HIS PRAISES

(any sudden, loud outburst or uproar of praise to God or a loud cry or call of joy declaring and describing how wonderful he is; God of My Praise)

1 Samuel 4:5

When the ark for the covenant of Adonai entered the camp, all Isra'el gave a mighty shout that resounded through the land.

2 Chronicles 20:19

And the L'vi'im from the descendants of the K'hati and the descendants of the Korchi stood up and praised Adonai the God of Isra'el at the top of their voices.

Psalm 5:12

But let all who take refuge in you rejoice, let them forever shout for joy!

Psalm 71:23

My lips will shout for joy; I will sing your praise, because you have redeemed me.

Psalm 89:16

How happy are the people who know the joyful shout! They walk in the light of your presence, Adonai.

Psalm 95:1

Come, let's sing to Adonai! Let's shout for joy to the Rock of our salvation!

Psalm 100:1

Shout for joy to Adonai, all the earth!

Isaiah 24:14

They lift their voices, singing for joy, shouting from the west to honor Adonai.

Luke 19:40

But he answered them, "I tell you that if they keep quiet, the stones will shout!"

Declaring Who He Is

*(to reveal, make clearly known, state, or announce openly
the many facets of the God of Abraham, Isaac, and Jacob)*

Deuteronomy 32:3

For I will proclaim the name of Adonai. Come, declare the greatness of our God!

Psalm 40:11

"I did not hide your righteousness in my heart but declared your faithfulness and salvation; I did not conceal your grace and truth from the great assembly."

Psalm 96:3

Declare his glory among the nations, his wonders among all peoples!

Isaiah 12:4

On that day you will say, "Give thanks to Adonai! Call on his name! Make his deeds known among the peoples, declare how exalted is his name."

1 Peter 2:9

But you are a chosen people, the King's cohanim, a holy nation, a people for God to possess! Why? In order for you to declare the praises of the One who called you out of darkness into his wonderful light.

Proclaiming His Word

(to boldly teach with authority, and make known everywhere the Living Torah)

Numbers 29:40

So Moses told the people of Israel everything just as the Lord had commanded Moses.

2 Chronicles 17:9

They taught in Y'hudah, having a scroll of the Torah of Adonai with them; they circulated through all the cities of Y'hudah, teaching among the people.

Psalm 19:8

The Torah of Adonai is perfect, restoring the inner person. The instruction of Adonai is sure, making wise the thoughtless.

Matthew 7:28–29

When Yeshua had finished saying these things, the crowds were amazed at the way he taught, for he was not instructing them like their Torah-teachers but as one who had authority himself.

Acts 4:29

"So now, Lord, take note of their threats; and enable your slaves to speak your message with boldness!"

Acts 8:4

However, those who were scattered announced the Good News of the word wherever they went.

1 Corinthians 9:17–19

For if I do this willingly, I have a reward; but if I do it unwillingly, I still do it, simply because I've been entrusted with a job. So then, what is my reward? Just this: that in proclaiming the Good News I can make it available free of charge, without making use of the rights to which it entitles me. For although I am a free man, not bound to do anyone's bidding, I have made myself a slave to all in order to win as many people as possible.

MAKING HIS NAME KNOWN

(to give a clear perception or understanding of Adonai and making others acquainted or familiar with his Wonderful Names)

1 Kings 8:43

"Then hear in heaven where you live, and act in accordance with everything about which the foreigner is calling to you; so that all the peoples of the earth will know your name and fear you, as does your people Isra'el, and so that they will know that this house which I have built bears your name."

Psalm 45:18

I will make your name known through all generations; thus the peoples will praise you forever and ever.

Psalm 76:2

In Y'hudah God is known; his name is great in Isra'el.

Psalm 105:1

Give thanks to Adonai! Call on his name! Make his deeds known among the peoples.

Isaiah 12:4

On that day you will say, "Give thanks to Adonai! Call on his name! Make his deeds known among the peoples, declare how exalted is his name."

John 17:6

"I made your name known to the people you gave me out of the world. They were yours, you gave them to me, and they have kept your word."

John 17:26

"I made your name known to them, and I will continue to make it known; so that the love with which you have loved me may be in them, and I myself may be united with them."

Remembering Him and His Wonders

(keeping in mind with deep awe, appreciation, joy, esteem, and gratitude who he is, what he has said, and what he has done; Lord God of the Hebrews)

Deuteronomy 7:18
Nevertheless, you are not to be afraid of them; you are to remember well what Adonai your God did to Pharoah and all of Egypt.

Psalm 22:28
All the ends of the earth will remember and turn to Adonai; all the clans of the nations will worship in your presence.

Psalm 77:12
So I will remind myself of Yah's doings; yes, I will remember your wonders of old.

Psalm 105:5
Remember the wonders he has done, his signs and his spoken rulings.

Psalm 143:5
I remember the days of old, reflecting on all your deeds, thinking about the work of your hands.

Ecclesiastes 12:1
So remember your creator while you are young, before the evil days come, and the years approach when you will say, "They no longer give me pleasure."

Isaiah 26:8
Following the way of your judgments, we put our hope in you. The desire of all our soul is to remember you and your name.

Isaiah 46:9
Remember things that happened at the beginning, long ago—that I am God, and there is no other; I am God, and there is none like me.

Revelation 3:3
So remember what you received and heard, and obey it, and turn from your sin!

Acknowledging Him

(to confess, or recognize God's authority and character, and to make it clearly evident by publicly agreeing with his Son; our Teacher)

1 Kings 8:33–34
"When your people Isra'el sin against you and in consequence are defeated by an enemy; then if they turn back to you, acknowledge your name, and pray and make their plea to you in this house; hear in heaven, forgive the sin of your people Isra'el, and bring them back to the land you gave to their ancestors."

Psalm 64:10
Everyone is awestruck—they acknowledge that it is God at work, they understand what he has done.

Proverbs 3:6
In all your ways acknowledge him; then he will level your paths.

Matthew 10:32
"Whoever acknowledges me in the presence of others I will also acknowledge in the presence of my Father in heaven."

Romans 10:9–10
That if you acknowledge publicly with your mouth that Yeshua is Lord and trust in your heart that God raised him from the dead, you will be delivered. For with the heart one goes on trusting and thus continues toward righteousness, while with the mouth one keeps on making public acknowledgment and thus continues toward deliverance."

Philippians 2:11
And every tongue will acknowledge that Yeshua the Messiah is Adonai—to the glory of God the Father.

Being Amazed at His Works

*(filled with surprise, wonder, and astonishment at the Enthroned One—
at what his hands have done, and how awesome and miraculous his works are)*

Deuteronomy 3:24

"O Lord God, you have only begun to show your servant your greatness and your mighty hand. For what god is there in heaven or on earth who can do such works and mighty acts as yours?"

Habakkuk 1:5

"Look among the nations, and see; wonder and be astounded. For I am doing a work in your days that you would not believe if told."

Matthew 9:33

After the demon was expelled the man who had been mute spoke, and the crowds were amazed. "Nothing like this has ever been seen in Isra'el," they said.

Matthew 15:31

The people were amazed as they saw mute people speaking, crippled people cured, lame people walking and blind people seeing; and they said a b'rakhah [blessing] to the God of Isra'el.

John 5:20

For the Father loves the Son and shows him everything he does; and he will show him even greater things than these, so that you will be amazed.

Acts 3:10

They recognized him as the same man who had formerly sat begging at the Beautiful Gate of the Temple, and they were utterly amazed and confounded at what had happened to him.

INDEX

OTHER RELATED RESOURCES

Available at Messianic Jewish Resources Int'l. • www.messianicjewish.net • 1-800-410-7367 • (Prices subject to change.)

Coming Soon!

Complete Jewish Study Bible - New Testament

- The New Testament portion of the Complete Jewish Bible, adapted for the American audience.
- Introductions and articles by well known Messianic Jewish theologians including Dr. David Friedman, Dr. John Fischer, Dr. Jeffrey Seif, Dr. Dan Juster, Rabbi Russ Resnik, and more.
-Hebrew Idioms found in the New Testament explained by Israeli Messianic Jewish scholar, Dr. David Friedman.

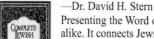

Complete Jewish Bible: *A New English Version*

—Dr. David H. Stern

Presenting the Word of God as a unified Jewish book, the *Complete Jewish Bible* is a new version for Jews and non-Jews alike. It connects Jews with the Jewishness of the Messiah, and non-Jews with their Jewish roots. Names and key terms are returned to their original Hebrew and presented in easy-to-understand transliterations, enabling the reader to say them the way Yeshua (Jesus) did! 1697 pages.

Hardback	**JB12**	$34.99	
Paperback	**JB13**	$29.99	
Leather Cover	**JB15**	$59.99	
Large Print (12 Pt font)	**JB16**	$49.99	Also available in French and Portuguese.

Jewish New Testament

—Dr. David H. Stern

The New Testament is a Jewish book, written by Jews, initially for Jews. Its central figure was a Jew. His followers were all Jews; yet no other version really communicates its original, essential Jewishness. Uses neutral terms and Hebrew names. Highlights Jewish references and corrects mistranslations. Freshly translated into English from Greek, this is a must read to learn about first-century faith. 436 pages

Hardback	**JB02**	$19.99	
Paperback	**JB01**	$14.99	Also available in French, German,
Spanish	**JB17**	$24.99	Polish, Portuguese and Russian.

Jewish New Testament Commentary

—Dr. David H. Stern

This companion to the *Jewish New Testament* enhances Bible study. Passages and expressions are explained in their original cultural context. 15 years of research. 960 pages.

Hardback	**JB06**	$34.99
Paperback	**JB10**	$29.99

Jewish New Testament on Audio CD or MP3

All the richness of the *Jewish New Testament* beautifully narrated in English by professional narrator/singer, Jonathan Settel. Thrilling to hear, you will enjoy listening to the Hebrew names, expressions and locations as spoken by Messiah.

20 CDs	**JC01**	$49.99
MP3	**JC02**	$49.99

Jewish New Testament & Commentary on CD-ROM

Do word searches, studies and more! And, because this is part of the popular LOGOS Bible program, you will have the "engine" to access one of the top Bible research systems. As an option, you'll be able to obtain and cross reference the Mishnah, Josephus, Bible dictionaries, and much more! Windows 3.1+ only.

JCD02	$39.99

Psalms & Proverbs *Tehillim* תְּהִלִּים - *Mishlei* מִשְׁלֵי

—Translated by Dr. David Stern

Contemplate the power in these words anytime, anywhere: Psalms-*Tehillim* offers uplifting words of praise and gratitude, keeping us focused with the right attitude; Proverbs-*Mishlei* gives us the wisdom for daily living, renewing our minds by leading us to examine our actions, to discern good from evil, and to decide freely to do the good. Makes a wonderful and meaningful gift. Softcover, 224 pages.

978-1936716692	LB90	$9.99

Messianic Judaism *A Modern Movement With an Ancient Past*

—David H. Stern

An updated discussion of the history, ideology, theology and program for Messianic Judaism. A challenge to both Jews and non-Jews who honor Yeshua to catch the vision of Messianic Judaism. 312 pages

LB62	$17.99

Restoring the Jewishness of the Gospel

A Message for Christians

—David H. Stern

Introduces Christians to the Jewish roots of their faith, challenges some conventional ideas, and raises some neglected questions: How are both the Jews and "the Church" God's people? Is the Law of Moses in force today? Filled with insight! Endorsed by Dr. Darrell L. Bock. 110 pages

English	**LB70**	$9.99
Spanish	**JB14**	$9.99

Under the Vine *Messianic Thought Through the Hebrew Calendar*
—Patrick Gabriel Lumbroso

Journey daily through the Hebrew Calendar and Biblical Feasts into the B'rit Hadashah (New Testament) Scriptures as they are put in their rightful context, bringing Judaism alive in it's full beauty. Messianic faith was the motor and what gave substance to Abraham's new beliefs, hope to Job, trust to Isaac, vision to Jacob, resilience to Joseph, courage to David, wisdom to Solomon, knowledge to Daniel, and divine Messianic authority to Yeshua. Softcover, 412 pages.

    978-1936716654   **LB87** $25.99

The Return of the Kosher Pig *The Divine Messiah in Jewish Thought*
—Rabbi Tzahi Shapira

The subject of Messiah fills many pages of rabbinic writings. Hidden in those pages is a little known concept that the Messiah has the same authority given to God. Based on the Scriptures and traditional rabbinic writings, this book shows the deity of Yeshua from a new perspective. You will see that the rabbis of old expected the Messiah to be divine. Softcover, 352 pages.

    978-1936716456   **LB81** $ 39.99

Come and Worship *Ways to Worship from the Hebrew Scriptures*
—Compiled by Barbara D. Malda

We were created to worship. God has graciously given us many ways to express our praise to him. Each way fits a different situation or moment in life, yet all are intended to bring honor and glory to him. When we believe that he is who he says he is [see *His Names are Wonderful!*] and that his Word is true, worship flows naturally from our hearts to his. Softcover, 128 pages.

    978-1936716678   **LB88** $9.99

His Names Are Wonderful

Getting to Know God Through His Hebrew Names
—Elizabeth L. Vander Meulen and Barbara D. Malda

In Hebrew thought, names did more than identify people; they revealed their nature. God's identity is expressed not in one name, but in many. This book will help readers know God better as they uncover the truths in his Hebrew names. 160 pages.

     LB58 $9.99

Stories of Yeshua

—Jim Reimann, Illustrator Julia Filipone-Erez

Children's Bible Storybook with four stories about Yeshua (Jesus).
Yeshua is Born: The Bethlehem Story based on Lk 1:26-35 & 2:1-20; *Yeshua and Nicodemus in Jerusalem* based on Jn 3:1-16; *Yeshua Loves the Little Children of the World* based on Matthew 18:1–6 & 19:13–15; *Yeshua is Alive-The Empty Tomb in Jerusalem* based on Matthew 26:17-56, Jn 19:16-20:18, Lk 24:50-53. Ages 3-7, Softcover, 48 pages.

    978-1936716685   **LB89** $14.99

Matthew Presents Yeshua, King Messiah *A Messianic Commentary*
—Rabbi Barney Kasdan

Few commentators are able to truly present Yeshua in his Jewish context. Most don't understand his background, his family, even his religion, and consequently really don't understand who he truly is. This commentator is well versed with first-century Jewish practices and thought, as well as the historical and cultural setting of the day, and the 'traditions of the Elders' that Yeshua so often spoke about. Get to know Yeshua, the King, through the writing of another rabbi, Barney Kasdan. 448 pages

LB76 $29.99

James the Just Presents Application of Torah

A Messianic Commentary

—Dr. David Friedman

James (Jacob) one of the Epistles written to first century Jewish followers of Yeshua. Dr. David Friedman, a former Professor of the Israel Bible Institute has shed new light for Christians from this very important letter.

978-1936716449   **LB82** $14.99

To the Ends of the Earth – How the First Jewish Followers of Yeshua Transformed the Ancient World

— Dr. Jeffrey Seif

Everyone knows that the first followers of Yeshua were Jews, and that Christianity was very Jewish for the first 50 to 100 years. It's a known fact that there were many congregations made up mostly of Jews, although the false perception today is, that in the second century they disappeared. Dr. Seif reveals the truth of what happened to them and how these early Messianic Jews influenced and transformed the behavior of the known world at that time.

978-1936716463   **LB83** $17.99

Passion for Israel: *A Short History of the Evangelical Church's Support of Israel and the Jewish People*
—Dan Juster

History reveals a special commitment of Christians to the Jews as God's still elect people, but the terrible atrocities committed against the Jews by so-called Christians have overshadowed the many good deeds that have been performed. This important history needs to be told to help heal the wounds and to inspire more Christians to stand together in support of Israel.

978-1936716401   **LB78** $9.99

On The Way to Emmaus: *Searching the Messianic Prophecies*
—Dr. Jacques Doukhan

An outstanding compilation of the most critical Messianic prophecies by a renowned conservative Christian Scholar, drawing on material from the Bible, Rabbinic sources, Dead Sea Scrolls, and more.

978-1936716432   **LB80** $14.99

The Red Heifer *A Jewish Cry for Messiah*
—Anthony Cardinale

Award-winning journalist and playwright Anthony Cardinale has traveled extensively in Israel, and recounts here his interviews with Orthodox rabbis, secular Israelis, and Palestinian Arabs about the current search for a red heifer by Jewish radicals wishing to rebuild the Temple and bring the Messiah. These real-life interviews are interwoven within an engaging and dramatic fictional portrayal of the diverse people of Israel and how they would react should that red heifer be found. Readers will find themselves in the Land, where they can hear learned rabbis and ordinary Israelis talking about the red heifer and dealing with all the related issues and the imminent coming and identity of Messiah.

978-1936716470	LB79	$19.99

Yeshua *A Guide to the Real Jesus and the Original Church*
—Dr. Ron Moseley

Opens up the history of the Jewish roots of the Christian faith. Illuminates the Jewish background of Yeshua and the Church and never flinches from showing "Jesus was a Jew, who was born, lived, and died, within first century Judaism." Explains idioms in the New Testament. Endorsed by Dr. Brad Young and Dr. Marvin Wilson. 213 pages.

	LB29	$12.99

Good News According To Matthew
—Dr. Henry Einspruch

English translation with quotations from the Tanakh (Old Testament) capitalized and printed in Hebrew. Helpful notations are included. Lovely black and white illustrations throughout the book. 86 pages.

	LB03	$4.99
Also available in Yiddish.	**LB02**	$4.99

The Gospels in their Jewish Context
—John Fischer, Th.D, Ph.D.

An examination of the Jewish background and nature of the Gospels in their contemporary political, cultural and historical settings, emphasizing each gospel's special literary presentation of Yeshua, and highlighting the cultural and religious contexts necessary for understanding each of the gospels. 32 hours of audio/video instruction on MP3-DVD and pdf of syllabus.

	LCD01	$49.99

The Epistles from a Jewish Perspective
—John Fischer, Th.D, Ph.D.

An examination of the relationship of Rabbi Shaul (the Apostle Paul) and the Apostles to their Jewish contemporaries and environment; surveys their Jewish practices, teaching, controversy with the religious leaders, and many critical passages, with emphasis on the Jewish nature, content, and background of these letters. 32 hours of audio/video instruction on MP3-DVD and pdf of syllabus.

	LCD02	$49.99

Gateways to Torah *Joining the Ancient Conversation on the Weekly Portion*
—Rabbi Russell Resnik

From before the days of Messiah until today, Jewish people have read from and discussed a prescribed portion of the Pentateuch each week. Now, a Messianic Jewish Rabbi, Russell Resnik, brings another perspective on the Torah, that of a Messianic Jew. 246 pages.

LB42	$15.99

Creation to Completion *A Guide to Life's Journey from the Five Books of Moses*
—Rabbi Russell Resnik

Endorsed by Coach Bill McCartney, Founder of Promise Keepers & Road to Jerusalem: "Paul urged Timothy to study the Scriptures (2 Tim. 3:16), advising him to apply its teachings to all aspects of his life. Since there was no New Testament then, this rabbi/apostle was convinced that his disciple would profit from studying the Torah, the Five Books of Moses, and the Old Testament. Now, Rabbi Resnik has written a warm devotional commentary that will help you understand and apply the Law of Moses to your life in a practical way." 256 pages

LB61	$14.99

Walk Genesis!
Walk Exodus!
Walk Leviticus!
Walk Numbers!
Walk Deuteronomy!

Messianic Jewish Devotional Commentaries
—Jeffrey Enoch Feinberg, Ph.D.

Using the weekly synagogue readings, Dr. Jeffrey Feinberg has put together some very valuable material in his "Walk" series. Each section includes a short Hebrew lesson (for the non-Hebrew speaker), key concepts, an excellent overview of the portion, and some practical applications. Can be used as a daily devotional as well as a Bible study tool.

Walk Genesis!	238 pages	**LB34**	$12.99
Walk Exodus!	224 pages	**LB40**	$12.99
Walk Leviticus!	208 pages	**LB45**	$12.99
Walk Numbers!	211 pages	**LB48**	$12.99
Walk Deuteronomy!	231 pages	**LB51**	$12.99
SPECIAL! Five-book Walk!	5 Book Set **Save $10**	**LK28**	$54.99

They Loved the Torah *What Yeshua's First Followers Really Thought About the Law*
—Dr. David Friedman

Although many Jews believe that Paul taught against the Law, this book disproves that notion. An excellent case for his premise that all the first followers of the Messiah were not only Torah-observant, but also desired to spread their love for God's entire Word to the gentiles to whom they preached. 144 pages. Endorsed by Dr. David Stern, Ariel Berkowitz, Rabbi Dr. Stuart Dauermann & Dr. John Fischer.

LB47 $9.99

The Distortion *2000 Years of Misrepresenting the Relationship Between Jesus the Messiah and the Jewish People*
—Dr. John Fischer & Dr. Patrice Fischer

Did the Jews kill Jesus? Did they really reject him? With the rise of global anti–Semitism, it is important to understand what the Gospels teach about the relationship between Jewish people and their Messiah. 2000 years of distortion have made this difficult. Learn how the distortion began and continues to this day and what you can do to change it. 126 pages. Endorsed by Dr. Ruth Fleischer, Rabbi Russell Resnik, Dr. Daniel C. Juster, Dr. Michael Rydelnik.

LB54 $11.99

---

eBooks Now Available!
All books are available as ebooks for your favorite reader

Visit www.messianicjewish.net for direct links
to these readers for each available eBook.

God's Appointed Times *A Practical Guide to Understanding and Celebrating the Biblical Holidays* – **New Edition.**
—Rabbi Barney Kasdan

The Biblical Holy Days teach us about the nature of God and his plan for mankind, and can be a source of God's blessing for all believers–Jews and Gentiles–today. Includes historical background, traditional Jewish observance, New Testament relevance, and prophetic significance, plus music, crafts and holiday recipes. 145 pages.

English	**LB63**	$12.99
Spanish	**LB59**	$12.99

God's Appointed Customs *A Messianic Jewish Guide to the Biblical Lifecycle and Lifestyle*
— Rabbi Barney Kasdan

Explains how biblical customs are often the missing key to unlocking the depths of Scripture. Discusses circumcision, the Jewish wedding, and many more customs mentioned in the New Testament. Companion to *God's Appointed Times*. 170 pages.

English	**LB26**	$12.99
Spanish	**LB60**	$12.99

Celebrations of the Bible *A Messianic Children's Curriculum*

Did you know that each Old Testament feast or festival finds its fulfillment in the New? They enrich the lives of people who experience and enjoy them. Our popular curriculum for children is in a brand new, user-friendly format. The lay-flat at binding allows you to easily reproduce handouts and worksheets. Celebrations of the Bible has been used by congregations, Sunday schools, ministries, homeschoolers, and individuals to teach children about the biblical festivals. Each of these holidays are presented for Preschool (2-K), Primary (Grades 1-3), Junior (Grades 4-6), and Children's Worship/Special Services. 208 pages.

LB55	$24.99

Passover: *The Key That Unlocks the Book of Revelation*
—Daniel C. Juster, Th.D.

Is there any more enigmatic book of the Bible than Revelation? Controversy concerning its meaning has surrounded it back to the first century. Today, the arguments continue. Yet, Dan Juster has given us the key that unlocks the entire book—the events and circumstances of the Passover/Exodus. By interpreting Revelation through the lens of Exodus, Dan Juster provides a unified overview that helps us read Revelation as it was always meant to be read, as a drama of spiritual conflict, deliverance, and above all, worship. He also shows how this final drama, fulfilled in Messiah, resonates with the Torah and all of God's Word. — Russ Resnik, Executive Director, Union of Messianic Jewish Congregations.

LB74	$10.99

The Messianic Passover Haggadah
Revised and Updated
—Rabbi Barry Rubin and Steffi Rubin.

Guides you through the traditional Passover seder dinner, step-by-step. Not only does this observance remind us of our rescue from Egyptian bondage, but, we remember Messiah's last supper, a Passover seder. The theme of redemption is seen throughout the evening. What's so unique about our Haggadah is the focus on Yeshua (Jesus) the Messiah and his teaching, especially on his last night in the upper room. 36 pages.

| English | **LB57** | $4.99 |
| Spanish | **LBSP01** | $4.99 |

The Messianic Passover Seder Preparation Guide
Includes recipes, blessings and songs. 19 pages.

| English | **LB10** | $2.99 |
| Spanish | **LBSP02** | $2.99 |

The Sabbath *Entering God's Rest*
—Barry Rubin & Steffi Rubin

Even if you've never celebrated Shabbat before, this book will guide you into the rest God has for all who would enter in—Jews and non-Jews. Contains prayers, music, recipes; in short, everything you need to enjoy the Sabbath, even how to observe havdalah, the closing ceremony of the Sabbath. Also discusses the Saturday or Sunday controversy. 48 pages.

| | **LB32** | $6.99 |

Havdalah *The Ceremony that Completes the Sabbath*
—Dr. Neal & Jamie Lash

The Sabbath ends with this short, yet equally sweet ceremony called havdalah (separation). This ceremony reminds us to be a light and a sweet fragrance in this world of darkness as we carry the peace, rest, joy and love of the Sabbath into the work week. 28 pages.

| | **LB69** | $4.99 |

Dedicate and Celebrate!
A Messianic Jewish Guide to Hanukkah
—Barry Rubin & Family

Hanukkah means "dedication" — a theme of significance for Jews and Christians. Discussing its historical background, its modern-day customs, deep meaning for all of God's people, this little book covers all the how-tos! Recipes, music, and prayers for lighting the menorah, all included! 32 pages.

| | **LB36** | $4.99 |

The Conversation *An Intimate Journal of the Emmaus Encounter*

—Judy Salisbury

"Then beginning with Moses and with all the prophets, He explained to them the things concerning Himself in all the Scriptures." Luke 24:27
If you've ever wondered what that conversation must have been like, this captivating book takes you there.

"The Conversation brings to life that famous encounter between the two disciples and our Lord Jesus on the road to Emmaus. While it is based in part on an imaginative reconstruction, it is filled with the throbbing pulse of the excitement of the sensational impact that our Lord's resurrection should have on all of our lives." ~ Dr. Walter Kaiser President Emeritus Gordon-Conwell Theological Seminary.
Hardcover 120 pages.

LB73	$14.99

Growing to Maturity

A Messianic Jewish Discipleship Guide

—Daniel C. Juster, Th.D.

This discipleship series presents first steps of understanding and spiritual practice, tailored for the Jewish believer. It's purpose is to aid the believer in living according to Yeshua's will as a disciple, one who has learned the example of his teacher. The course is structured according to recent advances in individualized educational instruction. Discipleship is serious business and the material is geared for serious study and reflection. Each chapter is divided into short sections followed by study questions. 256 pages.

LB75	$19.99

Growing to Maturity Primer: *A Messianic Jewish Discipleship Workbook*

—Daniel C. Juster, Th.D.

A basic book of material in question and answer form. Usable by everyone. 60 pages.

TB16	$7.99

Proverbial Wisdom & Common Sense

—Derek Leman

A Messianic Jewish Approach to Today's Issues from the Proverbs Unique in style and scope, this commentary on the book of Proverbs, written in devotional style, is divided into chapters suitable for daily reading. A virtual encyclopedia of practical advice on family, sex, finances, gossip, honesty, love, humility, and discipline. Endorsed by Dr. John Walton, Dr. Jeffrey Feinberg and Rabbi Barney Kasdan. 248 pages.

LB35	$14.99

That They May Be One *A Brief Review of Church Restoration Movements and Their Connection to the Jewish People*

—Daniel Juster, Th.D

Something prophetic and momentous is happening. The Church is finally fully grasping its relationship to Israel and the Jewish people. Author describes the restoration movements in Church history and how they connected to Israel and the Jewish people. Each one contributed in some way—some more, some less—toward the ultimate unity between Jews and Gentiles. Predicted in the Old Testament and fulfilled in the New, Juster believes this plan of God finds its full expression in Messianic Judaism. He may be right. See what you think as you read *That They May Be One*. 100 pages.

| | **LB71** | $9.99 |

The Greatest Commandment *How the Sh'ma Leads to More Love in Your Life*

—Irene Lipson

"What is the greatest commandment?" Yeshua was asked. His reply—"Hear, O Israel, the Lord our God, the Lord is one, and you are to love Adonai your God with all your heart, with all your soul, with all your understanding, and all your strength." A superb book explaining each word so the meaning can be fully grasped and lived. Endorsed by Elliot Klayman, Susan Perlman, & Robert Stearns. 175 pages.

| | **LB65** | $12.99 |

Blessing the King of the Universe

Transforming Your Life Through the Practice of Biblical Praise

—Irene Lipson

Insights into the ancient biblical practice of blessing God are offered clearly and practically. With examples from Scripture and Jewish tradition, this book teaches the biblical formula used by men and women of the Bible, including the Messiah; points to new ways and reasons to praise the Lord; and explains more about the Jewish roots of the faith. Endorsed by Rabbi Barney Kasdan, Dr. Mitch Glaser, & Rabbi Dr. Dan Cohn-Sherbok. 144 pages.

| | **LB53** | $11.99 |

You Bring the Bagels, I'll Bring the Gospel

Sharing the Messiah with Your Jewish Neighbor

Revised Edition—Now with Study Questions

—Rabbi Barry Rubin

This "how-to-witness-to-Jewish-people" book is an orderly presentation of everything you need to share the Messiah with a Jewish friend. Includes Messianic prophecies, Jewish objections to believing, sensitivities in your witness, words to avoid. A "must read" for all who care about the Jewish people. Good for individual or group study. Used in Bible schools. Endorsed by Harold A. Sevener, Dr. Walter C. Kaiser, Dr. Erwin J. Kolb and Dr. Arthur F. Glasser. 253 pages.

| English | **LB13** | $12.99 |
| Te Tengo Buenas Noticias | **OBSP02** | $14.99 |

Making Eye Contact With God
A Weekly Devotional for Women

—Terri Gillespie

What kind of eyes do you have? Are they downcast and sad? Are they full of God's joy and passion? See yourself through the eyes of God. Using real life anecdotes, combined with scripture, the author reveals God's heart for women everywhere, as she softly speaks of the ways in which women see God. Endorsed by prominent authors: Dr. Angela Hunt, Wanda Dyson and Kathryn Mackel. 247 pages, hardcover.

LB68 $19.99

Divine Reversal
The Transforming Ethics of Jesus

—Rabbi Russell Resnik

In the Old Testament, God often reversed the plans of man. Yeshua's ethics continue this theme. Following his path transforms one's life from within, revealing the source of true happiness, forgiveness, reconciliation, fidelity and love. From the introduction, "As a Jewish teacher, Jesus doesn't separate matters of theology from practice. His teaching is consistently practical, ethical, and applicable to real life, even two thousand years after it was originally given." Endorsed by Jonathan Bernis, Dr. Daniel C. Juster, Dr. Jeffrey L. Seif, and Dr Darrell Bock. 206 pages

LB72 $12.99

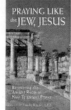

Praying Like the Jew, Jesus
Recovering the Ancient Roots of New Testament Prayer

—Dr. Timothy P. Jones

This eye-opening book reveals the Jewish background of many of Yeshua's prayers. Historical vignettes "transport" you to the times of Yeshua so you can grasp the full meaning of Messiah's prayers. Unique devotional thoughts and meditations, presented in down-to-earth language, provide inspiration for a more meaningful prayer life and help you draw closer to God. Endorsed by Mark Galli, James W. Goll, Rev. Robert Stearns, James F. Strange, and Dr. John Fischer. 144 pages.

LB56 $9.99

Growing Your Olive Tree Marriage *A Guide for Couples from Two Traditions*
—David J. Rudolph

One partner is Jewish; the other is Christian. Do they celebrate Hanukkah, Christmas or both? Do they worship in a church or a synagogue? How will the children be raised? This is the first book from a biblical perspective that addresses the concerns of intermarried couples, offering a godly solution. Includes highlights of interviews with intermarried couples. Endorsed by Walter C. Kaiser, Jr., Rabbi Dan Cohn-Sherbok, Jonathan Settel, Dr. Mitchell Glaser & Natalie Sirota. 224 pages.

LB50 $12.99

In Search of the Silver Lining *Where is God in the Midst of Life's Storms?*
—Jerry Gramckow

When faced with suffering, what are your choices? Storms have always raged. And people have either perished in their wake or risen above the tempests, shaping history by their responses…new storms are on the horizon. How will we deal with them? How will we shape history or those who follow us? The answer lies in how we view God in the midst of the storms. Endorsed by Joseph C. Aldrich, Ray Beeson, Dr. Daniel Juster. 176 pages.

LB39 $10.99

The Voice of the Lord *Messianic Jewish Daily Devotional*
—Edited by David J. Rudolph

Brings insight into the Jewish Scriptures—both Old and New Testaments. Twenty-two prominent Messianic contributors provide practical ways to apply biblical truth. Start your day with this unique resource. Explanatory notes. Perfect companion to the Complete Jewish Bible (see page 2). Endorsed by Edith Schaeffer, Dr. Arthur F. Glaser, Dr. Michael L. Brown, Mitch Glaser and Moishe Rosen. 416 pages.

LB31 $19.99

Kingdom Relationships *God's Laws for the Community of Faith*
—Dr. Ron Moseley

Dr. Ron Moseley's Yeshua: A Guide to the Real Jesus and the Original Church has taught thousands of people about the Jewishness of not only Yeshua, but of the first followers of the Messiah.

In this work, Moseley focuses on the teaching of Torah -- the Five Books of Moses -- tapping into truths that greatly help modern-day members of the community of faith.

The first section explains the relationship of both the Jewish people and Christians to the Kingdom of God. The second section lists the laws that are applicable to a non-Jew living in the twenty-first century and outside of the land of Israel.

This book is needed because these little known laws of God's Kingdom were, according to Yeshua, the most salient features of the first-century community of believers. Yeshua even warned that anyone breaking these laws would be least in the Kingdom (Matt. 5:19). Additionally, these laws will be the basis for judgment at the end of every believer's life. 64 pages.

LB37 $8.99

Train Up A Child *Successful Parenting For The Next Generation*
—Dr. Daniel L. Switzer

The author, former principal of Ets Chaiyim Messianic Jewish Day School, and father of four, combines solid biblical teaching with Jewish sources on child raising, focusing on the biblical holy days, giving fresh insight into fulfilling the role of parent. 188 pages. Endorsed by Dr. David J. Rudolph, Paul Lieberman, and Dr. David H. Stern.

LB64 $12.99

Fire on the Mountain - *Past Renewals, Present Revivals and the Coming Return of Israel*
—Dr. Louis Goldberg

The term "revival" is often used to describe a person or congregation turning to God. Is this something that "just happens," or can it be brought about? Dr. Louis Goldberg, author and former professor of Hebrew and Jewish Studies at Moody Bible Institute, examines real revivals that took place in Bible times and applies them to today. 268 pages.

LB38 $15.99

Voices of Messianic Judaism *Confronting Critical Issues Facing a Maturing Movement*
—General Editor Rabbi Dan Cohn-Sherbok

Many of the best minds of the Messianic Jewish movement contributed their thoughts to this collection of 29 substantive articles. Challenging questions are debated: The involvement of Gentiles in Messianic Judaism? How should outreach be accomplished? Liturgy or not? Intermarriage? 256 pages.

LB46 $15.99

The Enduring Paradox *Exploratory Essays in Messianic Judaism*
—General Editor Dr. John Fischer

Yeshua and his Jewish followers began a new movement—Messianic Judaism—2,000 years ago. In the 20th century, it was reborn. Now, at the beginning of the 21st century, it is maturing. Twelve essays from top contributors to the theology of this vital movement of God, including: Dr. Walter C. Kaiser, Dr. David H. Stern, and Dr. John Fischer. 196 pages.

LB43 $13.99

The World To Come *A Portal to Heaven on Earth*
—Derek Leman

An insightful book, exposing fallacies and false teachings surrounding this extremely important subject... paints a hopeful picture of the future and dispels many non-biblical notions. Intriguing chapters: Magic and Desire, The Vision of the Prophets, Hints of Heaven, Horrors of Hell, The Drama of the Coming Ages. Offers a fresh, but old, perspective on the world to come, as it interacts with the prophets of Israel and the Bible. 110 pages.

LB67   .$9.99

Hebrews Through a Hebrew's Eyes
—Dr. Stuart Sacks

Written to first-century Messianic Jews, this epistle, understood through Jewish eyes, edifies and encourages all. 119 pages. Endorsed by Dr. R.C. Sproul and James M. Boice.

LB23 $10.99

The Irrevocable Calling *Israel's Role As A Light To The Nations*
—Daniel C. Juster, Th.D.

Referring to the chosen-ness of the Jewish people, Paul, the Apostle, wrote "For God's free gifts and his calling are irrevocable" (Rom. 11:29). This messenger to the Gentiles understood the unique calling of his people, Israel. So does Dr. Daniel Juster, President of Tikkun Ministries Int'l. In *The Irrevocable Calling*, he expands Paul's words, showing how Israel was uniquely chosen to bless the world and how these blessings can be enjoyed today. Endorsed by Dr. Jack Hayford, Mike Bickle and Don Finto. 64 pages.

	LB66	$8.99

Are There Two Ways of Atonement?
—Dr. Louis Goldberg

Here Dr. Louis Goldberg, long-time professor of Jewish Studies at Moody Bible Institute, exposes the dangerous doctrine of Two-Covenant Theology. 32 pages.

	LB12	$ 4.99

Awakening *Articles and Stories About Jews and Yeshua*
—Arranged by Anna Portnov

Articles, testimonies, and stories about Jewish people and their relationship with God, Israel, and the Messiah. Includes the effective tract, "The Most Famous Jew of All." One of our best anthologies for witnessing to Jewish people. Let this book witness for you! Russian version also available. 110 pages.

English	**LB15**	$ 6.99
Russian	**LB14**	$ 6.99

The Unpromised Land *The Struggle of Messianic Jews Gary and Shirley Beresford*
—Linda Alexander

They felt God calling them to live in Israel, the Promised Land. Wanting nothing more than to live quietly and grow old together in the country of refuge for all Jewish people, little did they suspect what events would follow to try their faith. The fight to make *aliyah*, to claim their rightful inheritance in the Promised Land, became a battle waged not only for themselves, but also for Messianic Jews all over the world that wish to return to the Jewish homeland. Here is the true saga of the Beresford's journey to the land of their forefathers. 216 pages.

	LB19	$ 9.99

Death of Messiah *Twenty fascinating articles that address a subject of grief, hope, and ultimate triumph.*
—Edited by Kai Kjaer-Hansen

This compilation, written by well-known Jewish believers, addresses the issue of Messiah and offers proof that Yeshua—the true Messiah—not only died, but also was resurrected! 160 pages.

LB20 $ 8.99

Beloved Dissident *(A Novel)*
—Laurel West

A gripping story of human relationships, passionate love, faith, and spiritual testing. Set in the world of high finance, intrigue, and international terrorism, the lives of David, Jonathan, and Leah intermingle on many levels--especially their relationships with one another and with God. As the two men tangle with each other in a rising whirlwind of excitement and danger, each hopes to win the fight for Leah's love. One of these rivals will move Leah to a level of commitment and love she has never imagined--or dared to dream. Whom will she choose? 256 pages.

LB33 $ 9.99

Sudden Terror
—Dr. David Friedman

Exposes the hidden agenda of militant Islam. The author, a former member of the Israel Defense Forces, provides eye-opening information needed in today's dangerous world.

Dr. David Friedman recounts his experiences confronting terrorism; analyzes the biblical roots of the conflict between Israel and Islam; provides an overview of early Islam; demonstrates how the United States and Israel are bound together by a common enemy; and shows how to cope with terrorism and conquer fear. The culmination of many years of research and personal experiences. This expose will prepare you for what's to come! 160 pages.

LB49 $ 9.99

It is Good! *Growing Up in a Messianic Family*
—Steffi Rubin

Growing up in a Messianic Jewish family. Meet Tovah! Tovah (Hebrew for "Good") is growing up in a Messianic Jewish home, learning the meaning of God's special days. Ideal for young children, it teaches the biblical holidays and celebrates faith in Yeshua. 32 pages to read & color.

LB11 $ 4.99